Echoes Of
BAUDELAIRE

Nov/ 92.

Baudelaire is one
of the greatest French poets!

To Suzanne,
excellent student and
secretary.
With warmest wishes.

C. N. Fortis

ECHOES OF
Baudelaire

SELECTED POEMS

translated from the French
by

Kendall Lappin

with an introduction by
Greg Boyd

SANTA MARIA
ASYLUM ARTS
1992

ISBN 0-878580-28-0
ISBN 0-878580-27-2 (pbk.)

LC # 91-073680

Asylum Arts / P. O. Box 6203 / Santa Maria, CA 93456

Contents

Echoes of Baudelaire

Upon publication of *Les Fleurs du mal* in 1857, Charles Baudelaire was tried for and convicted of offending public morals and was fined 300 francs. Six poems in the collection were officially censored, cut out with scissors, from the first edition. "The whole volume is an asylum full of the inanities of the human mind, of all the putrescences of the human heart. All this would be permissible if its object were to cure them, but they are incurable," wrote one critic for *Le Figaro*, in an article which typified the literary establishment's response to the book.

Misunderstood and undervalued during his lifetime, Baudelaire's work continues to be misinterpreted by readers who revel in the intense portrayals of sin, vice, blasphemy and satanism, while ignoring or failing to perceive the overall spiritual quality of the collection. Though Baudelaire's quest for truth forced him to examine closely the evil in his own nature as well as that in society, he did find evidence of a spiritual side to man, even amid the horrors of experience. Despite the tremendous gulf between idealism and reality, Baudelaire nonetheless suggests that the very existence of the ideal provides hope for redemption. Through his art, the poet transforms his feelings of revulsion against sin and vice—along with his own self-loathing—into beauty: flowers of evil.

It is not surprising that many of Baudelaire's poems reflect the circumstances and events of his life. A sensitive, rebellious youth, he rejected the materialism of his powerful stepfather, General Aupick, and of the age itself, in choosing to become a poet. His family tried to persuade him to abandon this notion and pursue some conventional, respectable career. In 1841 they sent him off on a trip to India, hoping the experience of travel would promote their cause; but when his ship reached La Réunion in the Indian Ocean, he disembarked and made his way back to France. Upon coming of age and gaining control of a modest inheritance left him by his father, he set himself up not only as a man of letters but as a "dandy," determined to shock the bourgeois and to show his scorn for the stale and stodgy artistic tastes which prevailed in Paris during the reign of Louis Philippe.

During this period the poet occupied a suite of rooms in the Hôtel Lauzun, a historic mansion on the Ile St.-Louis. Living in all but idle luxury, he spent his money freely on outlandish clothes, works of art and other furnishings for his apartment, and entertainment, as well as on keeping his mulatto mistress, the actress Jeanne Duval, in suitably opulent surroundings. His days were more often filled with visits to museums and galleries, conversation with friends in the literary cafés, and attendance at theater performances than with serious devotion to professional writing. But the young Baudelaire's experiments with the sensual pleasures of wine, hashish, opium and women led to the end of his carefree existence: his extravagant lifestyle soon cost him his financial independence, while the syphilis he contracted at this time cast a lasting pall over his life and would eventually kill him.

Alarmed by his accumulating debts and the rapid depletion of his capital, Baudelaire's mother and stepfather sought and obtained a court order putting the remainder of his inheritance under the control of an appointed financial counselor, who was to disburse it to him in small monthly allotments. This proved devastating to Baudelaire, both practically and psychologically; he never managed to clear his debts, and he was never to feel free of financial pressures for the rest of his life.

Forced to give up the glamorous lifestyle of his youth, the ex-dandy Baudelaire now dressed in simple black suits, did what he could to placate his no-longer-pampered mistress, and pursued a career which was increasingly dictated by economic necessity or opportunity, and was therefore unfulfilling. But even during his worst financial difficulties, Baudelaire naively continued to believe that his efforts as a man of letters would, eventually, bring him financial rewards as well as the acclaim of his peers. In the course of his lifetime he produced both verse and prose poems, a good deal of commentary on art and literature, and a book dealing with the effects of hashish. Commercial success, however, was achieved only by his excellent translations of the works of Edgar Allan Poe into French.

In 1861-62, still hoping to win the esteem of his contemporaries, Baudelaire conducted an unrealistic campaign for election to the French Academy. Once again he was to be disappointed. The reaction of the Academy's members was unenthusiastic, even hostile; and after a period of just a few months, he withdrew his bid for a seat. His final humiliation came in the form of an ill-fated lecture tour to Belgium, where he delivered several talks which were poorly attended and unsuccessful. While still in Brussels, short on funds, discouraged by his inability to keep his work in print, and blocked at every turn from making new creative efforts, he fell seriously ill, eventually losing the capacity of speech.

After his return to France by train, in a private car paid for by some of his friends, Baudelaire became a patient in a Paris nursing home, where he died in August of 1867, aged forty-six. Soon thereafter a group of young poets, among them Verlaine and Rimbaud, acknowledged Baudelaire's influence on their development of a full-fledged Symbolist movement in French poetry, referring to him as "the Master."

The poems Baudelaire composed during his extravagant youth, representing as they do the fruits of his behavioral and artistic experimentation, are among the most shocking and blasphemous in *Les Fleurs du mal.* Poems such as "Les Bijoux," "Le Reniement de St. Pierre," "Au Lecteur" and "Le Mort joyeux," which express eroticism, rebellion against God, admiration for Satan, and a preoccupation with death and decay, evoked horror and disgust from his audience. While many readers see these elements as those most typical of Baudelaire's work, they are, as Enid Starkie points out in her biography of Baudelaire, equally characteristic of youth in general and of the literary fashions of the era. These poems, some of which have much in common with orthodox sermons about the consequences of sin, are indeed couched in a kind of confrontational language which is much less evident in the poet's later works.

By choosing to incorporate these early poems into his mature collection, Baudelaire deliberately highlighted the conflict which goes on constantly between man's spiritual aspirations and his base tendencies. The illumination of this conflict—the struggle between *Spleen* and *Idéal*—is central to an understanding of Baudelaire's work. While his depiction of vice is often seductive, the moral implications of the poems are clear: the individual who yields to human weakness and temptation must inevitably suffer remorse and self-loathing.

By the time *Les Fleurs du mal* was published, Baudelaire viewed himself as a moralist whose art served to illuminate man's struggle to remain virtuous in spite of the powerful attractions of vice. Starkie notes that the poet was amazed and deeply disturbed that others found his work immoral; for the aggressive and unfocused effusions of talent which mark his early work had solidified into a philosophic and moral system to which he was firmly committed. In writing to his mother in 1861 to protest against her confessor's having burned his book, Baudelaire complained that the cleric "didn't even understand that the book is based on a Catholic concept."

The poet professed that man must have knowledge of both good and evil, and that his capacity to feel shame and to recoil from evil elevates and ennobles him. Far from mistaking ugliness for beauty, as some have accused him of doing, Baudelaire found his own aversion to the horrors he portrayed to be uplifting and spiritually redeeming, and hence to be a fitting subject for artistic treatment. By evoking the proper reaction to evil—that of revulsion and disgust—Baudelaire shows the reader the best side of himself, not the worst. Like an alchemist working with base metals—the vileness of the modern city, the wretchedness all around him, the failings of his own spirit—the poet creates an art that is pure gold.

His intentions notwithstanding, Baudelaire, like many other artists since, was rejected by a public which vigorously resisted being shamed by his honesty. Like Joyce, Céline and Henry Miller after him, Baudelaire wrote in a way which disrupted people's smug, complacent illusions of human dignity, thereby bringing their wrath down upon him. Although public acceptance was important to him, the poet refused to compromise his vision to suit conventional morality. In preparing notes for his defense prior to the 1857 obscenity trial, he wrote: "Such a morality would mean that henceforth only comforting books should be written, with the purpose of proving that man is born good, and that all men are happy. What abominable hypocrisy!"

Whatever the moral implications of Baudelaire's work may be, whatever significance we may ascribe to the events of his life, the poet's work undeniably provides a torch with which to explore the darkest corners of human existence—and to shed light on whatever monsters lurk therein. In 1862, just five years before Baudelaire's death, the poet Alfred de Vigny, who was himself dying of cancer, wrote to Baudelaire that he had discovered the true essence and meaning of *Les Fleurs du mal*— a book which was, in his estimation, "too little appreciated as yet, and hitherto too superficially judged." The only major literary figure to recognize during the poet's lifetime the true nature of Baudelaire's work—a spiritual quest leading in the end, as great art must, to the revelation of truth—Vigny declared that "these *'fleurs du mal'* are, on the contrary, *'fleurs du bien.'"*

— Greg Boyd

FOREWORD

Poetry, being the most elevated, concentrated and musical form of literary expression, is quite naturally the most difficult to translate satisfactorily from one language to another. The complex interplay of poetic concept and imagery with such musical elements as rhythm and rhyme poses truly formidable obstacles to effective translation—so much so, in fact, that it has become the prevailing conventional wisdom to say that poetry cannot really be translated at all, but must instead be "poetically re-created."

This book, however, is offered as evidence to the contrary.[1] The selected Baudelaire poems presented here have been quite scrupulously translated, demonstrating that a conscientious translator, if he is sufficiently patient and discriminating, can achieve very satisfying results with certain types of poems without resorting to any "creative" departures from the poet's own thought.

What has been done here is based on a strategic approach featuring de-emphasis of rhyme in favor of rhythm. The strategy employed, as the reader will observe, is to disregard the rhyme-scheme entirely; to strive for strict semantic fidelity to what the poet actually says or clearly implies, without omission or substantive addition; and to emulate as effectively as possible the rhythm and flow of the lines. Its objectives, in the order of their importance, are: (1) to render faithfully both the sense and the spirit of the original; (2) to keep awkwardness and obscurity ("translatese") to a minimum; and (3) to preserve as much as possible of the music of each poem.

Over a period of many years, a great many individuals have tried their hand at rendering Baudelaire poems into English. Those translators whose versions are metrical in form tend to differ widely from one another in style, vocabulary, and degree of semantic accuracy; but almost all of them have in common

---

[1]See also the author's *Gallic Echoes*, Santa Maria, California: Asylum Arts Press, 1991.

two elements of technique: (1) they write for the most part in iambic meter; (2) all but one of them[2] contrive rhymes of their own in English, almost always conforming to the poet's rhyme-scheme. In my opinion, both of these procedural factors have adversely affected the results of their efforts.

The desirability of keeping the basic rhythmic beat of a poetic translation as similar as possible to that of its original is self-evident. If the two languages involved were similar in sound system and metrics, selection of the proper meter would be automatic; but this is not the case with French and English. The French poetic line, regardless of its length, normally has only one strong accent—on the last syllable; all other variations in stress are somewhat muted and subtle, so that no clear-cut intra-line metrical pattern is readily discernible. The English poetic line has relatively strong accents throughout; it is easier to analyze, and can be classified by type and number of metric feet. Most of Baudelaire's poems consist of twelve-syllable alexandrines; and these lines have a basic rhythm which can be approximated rather well in English by a flexible, often-de-fective[3] anapestic tetrameter. This four-foot line tends to maintain the flow of the French, precisely because it has relatively few accented syllables. The anapests (- - ´) move along lightly and easily, whereas the iambs (- ´) preferred by other translators, whether five to a line (pentameter) or six (hexam-eter), have a heavier cadence which has little in common with the fluid movement of Baudelaire's French.

The other key factor in implementation of this strategy, along with careful selection of meter, is deliberate abandonment of the rhyme-scheme. This is by no means merely "playing tennis with the net down"; it is a positive, enabling approach to the problem—an approach which has a perfectly sound ratio-nale, both aesthetic and practical in nature.

---

[2]The exception is Richard Howard, whose versions in *Les Fleurs du Mal, by Charles Baudelaire,* published by Godine of Boston in 1982, are non-rhyming.

[3]In anapestic tetrameter, an occasional defective (that is, iambic) foot tends to tighten or compress the line a bit. This is not unlike the effect of the counted-but-minimized mute *e*'s in a twelve-syllable French line.

From the standpoint of aesthetics, the most powerful argument against committing oneself to a fixed, predetermined rhyme-scheme is that such commitment inevitably complicates the rendition of content, and thereby impairs accuracy. It peremptorily assigns to the rhyme-scheme (an element of technique, not of substance) absolute priority over all other considerations. Baudelaire's many rhyming translators, in trying to accommodate the content of his poems to their own rhymes, have had to resort again and again to omission, addition and semantic distortion. Moreover, their rhymes themselves often sound artificial or labored; they seem to be primarily an intellectual *tour de force* on the part of the translator, rather than an integral element of poetic expression.

On the practical side, the translator must recognize the obvious impossibility of capturing in English, to any substantial degree, the rhyme-*music* of a French poem (as distinguished from its rhyme-*scheme*). No matter how ingenious the rhymes he or she may devise, they will not and cannot produce the same overall musical effect; for they will hardly ever *sound like* the French rhymes they replace. Their sequential arrangement or scheme (*a-b-b-a* or *a-b-a-b*, for example) can be made to correspond exactly to the poem's rhyme pattern; but that correspondence is purely spatial or systemic in nature—a superficial, essentially visual resemblance, which contributes very little to aural evocation of the French. Of course such substitute rhymes do provide a musicality of their own; but the overall "tune" they produce is not a familiar, evocative one, since virtually all of its component "notes" are different from the sounds of its model. With rare exceptions,[4] translators' rhymes do not echo, do not suggest aurally, the true rhyme-music of the original. In other words, they almost never accomplish the kind of musical emulation of the French poem which they are intended or presumed to accomplish.

Since the authentic effect of the poet's own rhyme-music cannot possibly be captured anyhow, there is very little of real

---

[4]Such welcome exceptions usually involve rhyming cognates. See for example my versions of "Le Goût du néant" (lines 7-8) and "La Béatrice" (lines 29-30).

value to be lost, and a great deal to be gained, by throwing off entirely the constraint of the rhyme-scheme. The translator who does so does not have to stretch and strain the poet's concepts and imagery, nor to "re-create" them, in order to make them fit into trumped-up rhymes of his own; on the contrary, he or she gains a great deal of freedom and flexibility, which can be put to good use in preserving the poem's content and its other characteristics, qualities and values. Meanwhile the deficit in atmospheric musicality can be reduced to some extent by the introduction of occasional (unpatterned) rhyme, near-rhyme, assonance, consonance, etc., whenever such musical devices are entirely compatible with sound metrical structure, semantic and tonal fidelity, and clarity and felicity of diction. These qualities, in my opinion, are far more essential to poetic translation than is scrupulous adherence to a rhyme-scheme, and should not be sacrificed for the sake of the latter.

It seems to me that good metrical structure, in particular, considerably enhances the effect of any incidental rhyme. This is especially true of a rhyme occurring in the closing lines of a poem, which creates a kind of residual "aural illusion" that rhyme has prevailed throughout.[5]

*   *   *

There are three individuals whose contributions to the completion of this project I wish to acknowledge with the utmost gratitude. The first is Henri Peyre, the famous French scholar and college professor, recently deceased. Dr. Peyre, an authority on Baudelaire in particular, was of great help to me on a regular basis; by graciously consenting to criticize in detail the accuracy of my translations, he enabled me to improve them continually by revision. The second is Greg Boyd, writer, artist, critic and publisher. Not only is Greg the author of the fore-going "Introduction: 'Les Fleurs du bien,'" but he also has

---

[5]See my versions of such poems as "Correspondances" and "Une Passante."

x

given me some very good advice with respect to the general tenor of this foreword. Last but not least is David Tomlinson of the Department of English, U.S. Naval Academy, a friend of long standing. Over an extended period, Dave has taken a strong interest in this project and has been most supportive, especially in providing me with a forum within his department.

— Kendall Lappin

Selections from
LES FLEURS DU MAL
(1861)

Au Lecteur

La sottise, l'erreur, le péché, la lésine,
Occupent nos esprits et travaillent nos corps,
Et nous alimentons nos aimables remords,
Comme les mendiants nourrissent leur vermine.

Nos péchés sont têtus, nos repentirs sont lâches;
Nous nous faisons payer grassement nos aveux,
Et nous rentrons gaiement dans le chemin bourbeux,
Croyant par de vils pleurs laver toutes nos taches.

Sur l'oreiller du mal c'est Satan Trismégiste
Qui berce longuement notre esprit enchanté,
Et le riche métal de notre volonté
Est tout vaporisé par ce savant chimiste.

C'est le Diable qui tient les fils qui nous remuent!
Aux objets répugnants nous trouvons des appas;
Chaque jour vers l'Enfer nous descendons d'un pas,
Sans horreur, à travers des ténèbres qui puent.

Ainsi qu'un débauché pauvre qui baise et mange
Le sein martyrisé d'une antique catin,
Nous volons au passage un plaisir clandestin
Que nous pressons bien fort comme une vieille orange.

Serré, fourmillant, comme un million d'helminthes,
Dans nos cerveaux ribote un peuple de Démons,
Et, quand nous respirons, la Mort dans nos poumons
Descend, fleuve invisible, avec de sourdes plaintes.

To the Reader

Stupidity, selfishness, error and sin
Belabor our bodies and prey on our minds,
And we lovingly feed our regrets and remorse
As verminous mendicants nurture their lice.

Our sins are ingrained, our repentances lax;
We exact for confessions a handsome reward,
And we blithely return to the path through the mire,
Expecting cheap tears to wash out all our stains.

On the pillow of evil it's Satan Thrice Great
Who constantly cradles our spirit enthralled,
And the metal, the strong tempered steel of our will
By that masterful chemist is turned into dust.

When we move, it's the Devil who's pulling the strings!
In the most loathsome things we discover some charm;
Every day we descend one more step toward Hell
Through a darkness that stinks, without horror or qualm.

Like an indigent lecher who kisses and bites
The martyrized breast of an elderly whore,
We casually steal some clandestine delight,
Which we squeeze very hard like a shriveled old orange.

Packed tightly and swarming like millions of worms,
A host of foul Demons carouse in our brains,
And whenever we breathe, Death flows down to our lungs,
An invisible river, with dull, hollow moans.

Si le viol, le poison, le poignard, l'incendie,
N'ont pas encor brodé de leurs plaisants dessins
Le canevas banal de nos piteux destins,
C'est que notre âme, hélas! n'est pas assez hardie.

Mais parmi les chacals, les panthères, les lices,
Les singes, les scorpions, les vautours, les serpents,
Les monstres glapissants, hurlants, grognants, rampants,
Dans la ménagerie infâme de nos vices,

Il en est un plus laid, plus méchant, plus immonde!
Quoiqu'il ne pousse ni grands gestes ni grands cris,
Il ferait volontiers de la terre un débris
Et dans un bâillement avalerait le monde;

C'est l'Ennui! — l'œil chargé d'un pleur involontaire,
Il rêve d'échafauds en fumant son houka.
Tu le connais, lecteur, ce monstre délicat,
— Hypocrite lecteur, — mon semblable, — mon frère!

If poisoning, fire-setting, stabbing and rape
Have not yet embroidered their striking designs
On the dráb counterpane of our pitiful lives,
It's just that, alas, we're too timid of soul!

But among the hyenas, the panthers, the hounds,
The monkeys, the scorpions, the vultures, the snakes,
All the slavering monsters that yap, howl and roar
In the infamous zoo of our vices, there's one

That is ugliest, filthiest, meanest of all!
Though it's sluggish of movement and utters no cries,
It would willingly make of the earth mere debris,
And would swallow the world in a single great yawn;

It's Ennui! — With an unconscious tear in its eye
And smoking its hookah, of gallows it dreams.
You know it, O reader, this monster effete,
— Hypocritical reader — my fellow — my twin!

from the cycle
"Spleen et idéal"

Bénédiction

Lorsque, par un décret des puissances suprêmes,
Le Poëte apparaît en ce monde ennuyé,
Sa mère épouvantée et pleine de blasphèmes
Crispe ses poings vers Dieu, qui la prend en pitié:

—"Ah! que n'ai-je mis bas tout un nœud de vipères,
Plutôt que de nourrir cette dérision!
Maudite soit la nuit aux plaisirs éphémères
Où mon ventre a conçu mon expiation!

Puisque tu m'as choisie entre toutes les femmes
Pour être le dégoût de mon triste mari,
Et que je ne puis pas rejeter dans les flammes,
Comme un billet d'amour, ce monstre rabougri,

Je ferai rejaillir ta haine qui m'accable
Sur l'instrument maudit de tes méchancetés,
Et je tordrai si bien cet arbre misérable,
Qu'il ne pourra pousser ses boutons empestés!"

Elle ravale ainsi l'écume de sa haine,
Et, ne comprenant pas les desseins éternels,
Elle-même prépare au fond de la Géhenne
Les bûchers consacrés aux crimes maternels.

Pourtant, sous la tutelle invisible d'un Ange,
L'Enfant déshérité s'enivre de soleil,
Et dans tout ce qu'il boit et dans tout ce qu'il mange
Retrouve l'ambroisie et le nectar vermeil.

Benediction

When, by some decree of the powers that be,
The Poet appears in this bored, weary world,
His mother, dismayed and with blasphemy filled,
Shakes her clenched fist at God, who takes pity on her:

"Ah, would I had borne a great tangle of snakes,
Rather than nurture this travesty vile!
Accursed be that night with its transient delights
When my belly conceived my atonement for sin!

Since of all the world's women you've singled out me
To fill my poor husband with grief and disgust,
And I can't throw this misshapen monster away,
As I would a love-letter, into the fire,

I shall turn all your hatred that overwhelms me
On the damned instrument of your malice and spite,
And so hard shall I twist this contemptible tree
That it never can put forth its foul, stinking buds!"

Thus she chokes back and swallows the foam of her hate,
And, not understanding the eternal designs,
By her own hand prepares in Gehenna's dark depths
The pyres dedicated to motherly crimes.

Nonetheless, in an Angel's invisible charge,
The derelict Child imbibes sunshine like wine,
And in all that he eats and in all that he drinks
Finds ambrosia and nectar like that of the gods.

Il joue avec le vent, cause avec le nuage,
Et s'enivre en chantant du chemin de la croix;
Et l'Esprit qui le suit dans son pèlerinage
Pleure de le voir gai comme un oiseau des bois.

Tous ceux qu'il veut aimer l'observent avec crainte,
Ou bien, s'enhardissant de sa tranquillité,
Cherchent à qui saura lui tirer une plainte,
Et font sur lui l'essai de leur férocité.

Dans le pain et le vin destinés à sa bouche
Ils mêlent de la cendre avec d'impurs crachats;
Avec hypocrisie ils jettent ce qu'il touche,
Et s'accusent d'avoir mis leurs pieds dans ses pas.

Sa femme va criant sur les places publiques:
"Puisqu'il me trouve assez belle pour m'adorer,
Je ferai le métier des idoles antiques,
Et comme elles je veux me faire redorer;

Et je me soûlerai de nard, d'encens, de myrrhe,
De génuflexions, de viandes et de vins,
Pour savoir si je puis dans un cœur qui m'admire
Usurper en riant les hommages divins!

Et, quand je m'ennuierai de ces farces impies,
Je poserai sur lui ma frêle et forte main;
Et mes ongles, pareils aux ongles des harpies,
Sauront jusqu'à son cœur se frayer un chemin.

Comme un tout jeune oiseau qui tremble et qui palpite,
J'arracherai ce cœur tout rouge de son sein,
Et, pour rassasier ma bête favorite,
Je le lui jetterai par terre avec dédain!"

He disports with the wind, holds converse with the clouds,
And feels rapture in chanting the Way of the Cross;
And the Spirit attending his journey through life
Is in tears to behold him as blithe as a bird.

All those he would love look upon him with fear,
Or else, waxing bold at his silence and calm,
Try to see who can cause him to cry out in pain,
And on him make the test of how cruel they can be.

The bread and the wine that are meant for his mouth
They sprinkle with ashes, with spittle befoul;
Whatever he touches they piously spurn,
And repent having stepped where his feet have once trod.

His woman proclaims to whoever will hear:
"Since my beauty so worthy of worship he finds,
Of antiquity's idols I'll play the old game,
And like them I shall have myself gilded anew;

And I'll revel in spikenard, in incense and myrrh,
In meek genuflections, in viands and wines,
Just to see if I can, in a heart that loves me,
Usurp, for a laugh, its devotion to God!

And when I grow tired of this impious farce,
I shall then lay upon him my frail, potent hand,
And my nails, like the harpies' redoubtable claws,
Will dig their way forcibly right to his heart.

That heart, like a fluttering, trembling young bird,
I shall tear out all crimson and raw from his breast,
And to gorge to repletion my precious pet dog,
I shall throw it disdainfully down on the ground!"

Vers le Ciel, où son œil voit un trône splendide,
Le Poëte serein lève ses bras pieux,
Et les vastes éclairs de son esprit lucide
Lui dérobent l'aspect des peuples furieux:

—"Soyez béni, mon Dieu, qui donnez la souffrance
Comme un divin remède à nos impuretés
Et comme la meilleure et la plus pure essence
Qui prépare les forts aux saintes voluptés!

Je sais que vous gardez une place au Poëte
Dans les rangs bienheureux des saintes Légions,
Et que vous l'invitez à l'éternelle fête
Des Trônes, des Vertus, des Dominations.

Je sais que la douleur est la noblesse unique
Où ne mordront jamais la terre et les enfers,
Et qu'il faut pour tresser ma couronne mystique
Imposer tous les temps et tous les univers.

Mais les bijoux perdus de l'antique Palmyre,
Les métaux inconnus, les perles de la mer,
Par votre main montés, ne pourraient pas suffire
A ce beau diadème éblouissant et clair;

Car il ne sera fait que de pure lumière,
Puisée au foyer saint des rayons primitifs,
Et dont les yeux mortels, dans leur splendeur entière,
Ne sont que des miroirs obscurcis et plaintifs!"

Toward Heaven, where his eye sees a glorious throne,
The Poet serene lifts his reverent arms,
And the far-flashing gleams of his spirit's clear flame
Make him blind to his fellow-man's furious glares:

—"Be blessèd, O God, you who suffering give
As a physic divine for our grossness and flaws,
And the purest and best of all essences rare,
Which readies the strong for beatified bliss!

I know that you keep for the Poet a place
In the thrice-blessed ranks of the Legions of Saints,
And eternal rejoicing invite him to share
With the choirs of the Virtues, Dominions and Thrones.

I know that affliction's the only noblesse
Which the earth and all Hades can never corrode,
And that weaving my mystical crown must impose
On all aeons of time and the whole universe.

But not all of ancient Palmyra's lost gems,
The rare precious metals, the pearls of the sea,
Enchased by your very own hand, would suffice
For that beautiful diadem dazzling and bright;

For it will be made of naught else but pure light
From the sacred fount dipped, from the source of prime rays,
And of which mortal eyes, in their splendor entire,
Are no more than mirrors, plaintive and bedimmed!"

L'Albatros

Souvent, pour s'amuser, les hommes d'équipage
Prennent des albatros, vastes oiseaux des mers,
Qui suivent, indolents compagnons de voyage,
Le navire glissant sur les gouffres amers.

A peine les ont-ils déposés sur les planches,
Que ces rois de l'azur, maladroits et honteux,
Laissent piteusement leurs grandes ailes blanches
Comme des avirons traîner à côté d'eux.

Ce voyageur ailé, comme il est gauche et veule!
Lui, naguère si beau, qu'il est comique et laid!
L'un agace son bec avec un brûle-gueule,
L'autre mime, en boitant, l'infirme qui volait!

Le Poëte est semblable au prince des nuées
Qui hante la tempête et se rit de l'archer;
Exilé sur le sol, au milieu des huées,
Ses ailes de géant l'empêchent de marcher.

The Albatross

Sailors, ofttimes, for amusement or sport,
Will capture an albatross, hugest of sea-birds,
Whose kind follow idly, companionably,
After ships as they skim the salt deeps of the sea.

No sooner deposed on the planks of the deck
Than this king of the blue, awkward now and ashamed,
Lets droop piteously his great snow-white wings,
Dragging them stiffly like oars at his sides.

This tireless winged nomad—how clumsy and weak!
Where now is his beauty? He's ugly, absurd!
With a cutty pipe one sailor pokes at his beak;
Another mocks, limping, the cripple who soared!

The Poet resembles this prince of the clouds,
Who seeks out the storm and makes light of the shaft;
Marooned on the ground, amid jeers and catcalls,
His vast giant's wings make him stumble and fall.

Elévation

Au-dessus des étangs, au-dessus des vallées,
Des montagnes, des bois, des nuages, des mers,
Par delà le soleil, par delà les éthers,
Par delà les confins des sphères étoilées,

Mon esprit, tu te meus avec agilité,
Et, comme un bon nageur qui se pâme dans l'onde,
Tu sillonnes gaiement l'immensité profonde
Avec une indicible et mâle volupté.

Envole-toi bien loin de ces miasmes morbides;
Va te purifier dans l'air supérieur,
Et bois, comme une pure et divine liqueur,
Le feu clair qui remplit les espaces limpides.

Derrière les ennuis et les vastes chagrins
Qui chargent de leur poids l'existence brumeuse,
Heureux celui qui peut d'une aile vigoureuse
S'élancer vers les champs lumineux et sereins;

Celui dont les pensers, comme des alouettes,
Vers les cieux le matin prennent un libre essor,
—Qui plane sur la vie, et comprend sans effort
Le langage des fleurs et des choses muettes!

Elevation

Above ponds and lakes, above valleys and dales,
Above mountains and forests and clouds and the seas,
Past the sun, to ethereal space and beyond,
Beyond the confines of the star-spangled spheres,

My spirit, you move with alacritous ease,
And like a good swimmer who basks in the wave,
You delightedly furrow the infinite deep
With a virile, ineffably sensual joy.

From these morbid miasmas fly far, far away;
Go and make yourself pure in the high upper air,
And imbibe, like an untainted nectar divine,
The bright glow that pervades the clear reaches of space.

From behind the great mass of afflictions and woes
That encumber this earthly existence opaque,
Most fortunate he who on powerful wings
Can soar upward to meadows of luminous calm;

He whose thoughts in the morning, like midsummer larks,
In freedom take flight to the heavens above,
—Who can float above life, and with ease comprehend
The language of flowers and of all voiceless things!

Correspondances

La Nature est un temple où de vivants piliers
Laissent parfois sortir de confuses paroles;
L'homme y passe à travers des forêts de symboles
Qui l'observent avec des regards familiers.

Comme de longs échos qui de loin se confondent
Dans une ténébreuse et profonde unité,
Vaste comme la nuit et comme la clarté,
Les parfums, les couleurs et les sons se répondent.

Il est des parfums frais comme des chairs d'enfants,
Doux comme les hautbois, verts comme les prairies,
—Et d'autres, corrompus, riches et triomphants,

Ayant l'expansion des choses infinies,
Comme l'ambre, le musc, le benjoin et l'encens
Qui chantent les transports de l'esprit et des sens.

Correspondences

All Nature's a temple whose pillars, alive,
Sometimes utter words indistinct and unclear;
Man passes through forests of symbols therein
Which observe him with knowing, familiar regards.

Like lingering echoes that blend from afar
Into incomprehensible oneness profound,
Immense as the night and the clear light of day,
Fragrances, colors and sounds correspond.

There are scents fresh and cool like the flesh of a child,
Clear and dulcet like oboes, soft green like the fields,
—And others, corrupt, overpowering and rich,

That have the expansion of infinite things,
Such as ambergris, benjamin, musk and incense,
Which sing of the transports of spirit and sense.

Les Phares

Rubens, fleuve d'oubli, jardin de la paresse,
Oreiller de chair fraîche où l'on ne peut aimer,
Mais où la vie afflue et s'agite sans cesse,
Comme l'air dans le ciel et la mer dans la mer;

Léonard de Vinci, miroir profond et sombre,
Où des anges charmants, avec un doux souris
Tout chargé de mystère, apparaissent à l'ombre
Des glaciers et des pins qui ferment leur pays;

Rembrandt, triste hôpital tout rempli de murmures,
Et d'un grand crucifix décoré seulement,
Où la prière en pleurs s'exhale des ordures,
Et d'un rayon d'hiver traversé brusquement;

Michel-Ange, lieu vague où l'on voit des Hercules
Se mêler à des Christs, et se lever tout droits
Des fantômes puissants qui dans des crépuscules
Déchirent leur suaire en étirant leurs doigts;

Colères de boxeur, impudences de faune,
Toi qui sus ramasser la beauté des goujats,
Grand cœur gonflé d'orgueil, homme débile et jaune,
Puget, mélancolique empereur des forçats;

Watteau, ce carnaval où bien des cœurs illustres,
Comme des papillons, errent en flamboyant,
Décors frais et légers éclairés par des lustres
Qui versent la folie à ce bal tournoyant;

The Beacons

Rubens, Lethe's river, lazy garden of ease,
Freshened pillow of flesh where one cannot make love
But where life teems and surges and ceaselessly stirs,
Like the winds in the air and the tides in the sea;

Leonardo da Vinci, dark mirror and deep,
Where angels enchanting, with sweet gentle smiles
Enigmatic, appear against backgrounds composed
Of the snow-fields and pines which their homeland enclose;

Rembrandt, sad hospital filled with soft moans
And by one great crucifix solely adorned,
Where prayer is exhaled from the refuse in tears,
And brusquely traversed by a wintry sun's ray;

Michelangelo, limbo where muscular Greeks
Intermingle with Christs, and where powerful ghosts
Are seen rising up straight in a murky half-light
And with tense, straining fingers, tearing their shrouds;

A prize-fighter's anger, a faun's impudence,
You who knew how to capture the beauty of churls,
Great pride-swollen heart in a weak, jaundiced man,
Puget, gloomy emperor of convicts in chains;

Watteau, carnival where illustrious souls
In great number like flamboyant butterflies flit,
Light and airy decors lit by great chandeliers,
Which shed a mad glow on this whirling dress-ball;

Goya, cauchemar plein de choses inconnues,
De fœtus qu'on fait cuirc au milieu des sabbats,
De vieilles au miroir et d'enfants toutes nues,
Pour tenter les démons ajustant bien leurs bas;

Delacroix, lac de sang hanté des mauvais anges,
Ombragé par un bois de sapins toujours vert,
Où, sous un ciel chagrin, des fanfares étranges
Passent, comme un soupir étouffé de Weber;

Ces malédictions, ces blasphèmes, ces plaintes,
Ces extases, ces cris, ces pleurs, ces *Te Deum*,
Sont un écho redit par mille labyrinthes;
C'est pour les cœurs mortels un divin opium!

C'est un cri répété par mille sentinelles,
Un ordre renvoyé par mille porte-voix;
C'est un phare allumé sur mille citadelles,
Un appel de chasseurs perdus dans les grands bois!

Car c'est vraiment, Seigneur, le meilleur témoignage
Que nous puissions donner de notre dignité
Que cet ardent sanglot qui roule d'âge en âge
Et vient mourir au bord de votre éternité!

Goya, eerie nightmare of things never known,
Of fœtuses cooking in witch-sabbath pots,
Of hags at the mirror and nude little girls
Adjusting their stockings the demons to tempt;

Delacroix, lake of blood where the bad angels throng,
Set within a dark forest of evergreen pines,
Where beneath a bleak sky, strange and wondrous brass bands
Pass along, like a muffled, suppressed Weber sigh;

These curses, these blasphemies, wailings and moans,
These ecstasies, outcries, *Te Deum*'s and tears,
Are a thousandfold echo from labyrinth walls;
For all mortal hearts, it's an opium divine!

It's a password repeated by thousands of guards,
An order through thousands of megaphones barked;
It's a beacon on thousands of citadels fired,
A distress call from hunters lost deep in the woods!

For it's truly, O Lord, the best evidence
We could possibly give of our worth here on earth—
This great ardent sob which from age rolls to age
And at last comes to Thee, on eternity's shore!

Le Mauvais Moine

Les cloîtres anciens sur leurs grandes murailles
Etalaient en tableaux la sainte Vérité,
Dont l'effet, réchauffant les pieuses entrailles,
Tempérait la froideur de leur austérité.

En ces temps où du Christ florissaient les semailles,
Plus d'un illustre moine, aujourd'hui peu cité,
Prenant pour atelier le champ des funérailles,
Glorifiait la Mort avec simplicité.

—Mon âme est un tombeau que, mauvais cénobite,
Depuis l'éternité je parcours et j'habite;
Rien n'embellit les murs de ce cloître odieux.

O moine fainéant! quand saurai-je donc faire
Du spectacle vivant de ma triste misère
Le travail de mes mains et l'amour de mes yeux?

The Bad Monk

Monasteries of old, on their great inner walls,
Used to show forth in paintings the scriptural Truth,
Which by warming the pious insides of the monks
Served to temper the cold of their austerity.

In those times when the seeds of the Christ grew apace,
More than one worthy monk, little noted today,
Taking burial-grounds for his workshop in stone,
Used to celebrate Death with devout naïveté.

—My soul is a tomb which, a bad cenobite,
I have trodden and dwelt in since time first began;
Yet the walls of this odious cloister are bare.

Idle monk that I am! When then shall I learn
To make of my wretchedness' live horror-show
The work of my hands and the love of my eyes?

L'Ennemi

Ma jeunesse ne fut qu'un ténébreux orage,
Traversé çà et là par de brillants soleils;
Le tonnerre et la pluie ont fait un tel ravage,
Qu'il reste en mon jardin bien peu de fruits vermeils.

Voilà que j'ai touché l'automne des idées,
Et qu'il faut employer la pelle et les râteaux
Pour rassembler à neuf les terres inondées,
Où l'eau creuse des trous grands comme des tombeaux.

Et qui sait si les fleurs nouvelles que je rêve
Trouveront dans ce sol lavé comme une grève
Le mystique aliment qui ferait leur vigueur?

—O douleur! ô douleur! Le Temps mange la vie,
Et l'obscure Ennemi qui nous ronge le cœur
Du sang que nous perdons croît et se fortifie!

The Foe

My youth was naught else but a dark, raging storm,
Traversed here and there by a ray of bright sun;
The thunder and rain wrought such havoc and harm
That but few crimson fruits in my garden remain.

Now it seems I have reached the autumn of ideas,
And must use in that garden the spade and the rake
To make whole once again the inundated ground,
Where the water has hollowed out holes big as graves.

And who knows if the new blooms I'm now dreaming of
Will find in this soil, washed and leached like a strand,
The mystical food which would cause them to thrive?

O sorrow! O grief! Life is eaten by Time,
And the dark, deadly Foe who still gnaws at our hearts,
From the blood that we lose, grows gigantic and strong!

Le Guignon

Pour soulever un poids si lourd,
Sisyphe, il faudrait ton courage!
Bien qu'on ait du cœur à l'ouvrage,
L'Art est long et le Temps est court.

Loin des sépultures célèbres,
Vers un cimetière isolé,
Mon cœur, comme un tambour voilé,
Va battant des marches funèbres.

—Maint joyau dort enseveli
Dans les ténèbres et l'oubli,
Bien loin des pioches et des sondes;

Mainte fleur épanche à regret
Son parfum doux comme un secret
Dans les solitudes profondes.

Ill-Starred

To lift and bear so great a weight
Would take thy courage, Sisyphus!
Although one's heart be in the task,
Art is long and Time is short.

Far from glory's sepulchers,
Toward some burial-ground remote,
My heart now, like a muffled drum,
Keeps beating out a funeral march.

Many a jewel buried sleeps
In darkness and oblivion,
Beyond the reach of pick or plumb;

Many a flower reluctantly
Wafts forth its secret-sweet perfume
In lonely deserts vast and deep.

La Vie antérieure

J'ai longtemps habité sous de vastes portiques
Que les soleils marins teignaient de mille feux,
Et que leurs grands piliers, droits et majestueux,
Rendaient pareils, le soir, aux grottes basaltiques.

Les houles, en roulant les images des cieux,
Mêlaient d'une façon solennelle et mystique
Les tout-puissants accords de leur riche musique
Aux couleurs du couchant reflété par mes yeux.

C'est là que j'ai vécu dans les voluptés calmes,
Au milieu de l'azur, des vagues, des splendeurs
Et des esclaves nus, tout imprégnés d'odeurs,

Qui me rafraîchissaient le front avec des palmes,
Et dont l'unique soin était d'approfondir
Le secret douloureux qui me faisait languir.

The Previous Life

For a long time I dwelt beneath vast porticoes
Which the suns and the sea tinged with myriad fires,
And whose columns majestic, so straight and so tall,
Made them look like, at evening, basaltic grottoes.

The long swells, reflecting the skies as they rolled,
Would blend, in a solemn and mystical way,
The all-powerful chords of their music so rich
With the hues of the sunset my eyes mirrored there.

It was there that I lived in voluptuous calm,
Amid blue skies, and waves, and rich splendors galore,
And attended by highly-perfumed naked slaves,

Who would cool my brow for me with fronds of the palm,
And whose one great concern was to try to divine
The dolorous secret that caused me to pine.

Bohémiens en voyage

La tribu prophétique aux prunelles ardentes
Hier s'est mise en route, emportant ses petits
Sur son dos, ou livrant à leurs fiers appétits
Le trésor toujours prêt des mamelles pendantes.

Les hommes vont à pied sous leurs armes luisantes
Le long des chariots où les leurs sont blottis,
Promenant sur le ciel des yeux appesantis
Par le morne regret des chimères absentes.

Du fond de son réduit sablonneux, le grillon,
Les regardant passer, redouble sa chanson;
Cybèle, qui les aime, augmente ses verdures,

Fait couler le rocher et fleurir le désert
Devant ces voyageurs, pour lesquels est ouvert
L'empire familier des ténèbres futures.

Gypsies on the Move

The prophetical tribe with the burning dark eyes
Took the road yesterday with their babes pickaback,
Or regaling their fine hearty appetites with
The convenient treasure of pendulous breasts.

Bearing weapons agleam, the men stride alongside
The wagons that shelter the ones they hold dear,
Ever scanning the skies with eyes heavy and sad,
As if mourning the absence of visions now fled.

The cricket, from deep in his sandy redoubt,
As he watches their passing, redoubles his song;
Cybele, who loves them, her verdure augments,

Makes the rock to gush water, the desert to bloom
For these wanderers with access, familiar and free,
To the future's obscure and inscrutable realm.

L'Homme et la Mer

Homme libre, toujours tu chériras la mer!
La mer est ton miroir; tu contemples ton âme
Dans le déroulement infini de sa lame,
Et ton esprit n'est pas un gouffre moins amer.

Tu te plais à plonger au sein de ton image;
Tu l'embrasses des yeux et des bras, et ton cœur
Se distrait quelquefois de sa propre rumeur
Au bruit de cette plainte indomptable et sauvage.

Vous êtes tous les deux ténébreux et discrets:
Homme, nul n'a sondé le fond de tes abîmes,
O mer, nul ne connaît tes richesses intimes,
Tant vous êtes jaloux de garder vos secrets.

Et cependant voilà des siècles innombrables
Que vous vous combattiez sans pitié ni remord,
Tellement vous aimez le carnage et la mort,
O lutteurs éternels, ô frères implacables!

Man and the Sea

Free man, you forever will cherish the sea!
The sea is your mirror; you behold your own soul
In the infinite rolling and sweep of her wave,
And your mind is a gulf no less bitter and deep.

You enjoy plunging into your counterpart's breast;
You embrace her with eyes and with arms, and your heart
Is distracted at times from its own pounding beat
By the sound of that murmur so fierce and untamed.

Both of you are mysterious, secretive, discreet;
O man, none has fathomed the depths you can sink to;
O sea, no one knows what rich treasures you hold,
So jealous you are, your dark secrets to keep.

And yet for numberless centuries past
You have fought one another sans pity or qualm,
So much do you love dealing carnage and death,
O eternal combatants, implacable twins!

La Beauté

Je suis belle, ô mortels! comme un rêve de pierre,
Et mon sein, où chacun s'est meurtri tour à tour,
Est fait pour inspirer au poète un amour
Eternel et muet ainsi que la matière.

Je trône dans l'azur comme un sphinx incompris;
J'unis un cœur de neige à la blancheur des cygnes;
Je hais le mouvement qui déplace les lignes,
Et jamais je ne pleure et jamais je ne ris.

Les poètes, devant mes grandes attitudes,
Que j'ai l'air d'emprunter aux plus fiers monuments,
Consumeront leurs jours en d'austères études;

Car j'ai, pour fasciner ces dociles amants,
De purs miroirs qui font toutes choses plus belles:
Mes yeux, mes larges yeux aux clartés éternelles!

Beauty

I'm beautiful, O mortals! like a dream in stone,
And my breast, where each one has been bruised in his turn,
Is fashioned to inspire the poet with a love
As mute and as eternal as the stone itself.

I sit in azure state, like an unfathomed sphinx;
I join a heart of snow to swans' unsullied white;
I abhor movement, which displaces lovely lines,
And never do I laugh and never do I weep.

Poets, confronted by my striking attitudes,
Which I seem to borrow from proudest monuments,
Will waste their lives in solemn study of me; for

I have, with which to charm these docile paramours,
Pure mirrors rendering all things more beautiful:
My eyes, my two wide eyes with lights forever bright!

La Géante

Du temps que la Nature en sa verve puissante
Concevait chaque jour des enfants monstrueux,
J'eusse aimé vivre auprès d'une jeune géante,
Comme aux pieds d'une reine un chat voluptueux.

J'eusse aimé voir son corps fleurir avec son âme
Et grandir librement dans ses terribles jeux;
Deviner si son cœur couve une sombre flamme
Aux humides brouillards qui nagent dans ses yeux;

Parcourir à loisir ses magnifiques formes;
Ramper sur le versant de ses genoux énormes,
Et parfois en été, quand les soleils malsains,

Lasse, la font s'étendre à travers la campagne,
Dormir nonchalamment à l'ombre de ses seins,
Comme un hameau paisible au pied d'une montagne.

The Giantess

In the time when Nature, in her power and zest,
Used to conceive each day some sort of monster-child,
I would have liked to live with a young giantess,
Like a voluptuous cat at the feet of a queen.

I would have liked to see her bloom, body and soul,
And grow up free, enjoying her prodigious games;
To guess if some dark flame was smouldering in her heart
By watching the damp mists that floated in her eyes;

To roam at will upon her parts magnificent,
To clamber up and down in her enormous lap,
And sometimes in summer when, tired by baneful sun,

She lay down at full length across the countryside,
To sleep insouciant in her great bosoms' shade,
Like a peaceful hamlet at a mountain's foot.

Parfum exotique

Quand, les deux yeux fermés, en un soir chaud d'automne,
Je respire l'odeur de ton sein chaleureux,
Je vois se dérouler des rivages heureux
Qu'éblouissent les feux d'un soleil monotone;

Une île paresseuse où la nature donne
Des arbres singuliers et des fruits savoureux;
Des hommes dont le corps est mince et vigoureux,
Et des femmes dont l'œil par sa franchise étonne.

Guidé par ton odeur vers de charmants climats,
Je vois un port rempli de voiles et de mâts
Encor tout fatigués par la vague marine,

Pendant que le parfum des verts tamariniers,
Qui circule dans l'air et m'enfle la narine,
Se mêle dans mon âme au chant des mariniers.

Exotic Perfume

When with my two eyes closed, on a warm autumn eve,
I breathe the odor of your bosom warm and sweet,
I see unfold a vision of a blissful shore
Ashimmer in the blaze of an unfailing sun;

A lazy, languid isle where Nature lavishes
A wealth of curious trees and savory strange fruits;
Where live strong-bodied men, slim, lithe and vigorous,
And women who surprise by the candor of their eyes.

Led by your odor to delightful distant climes,
I see a busy harbor filled with sails and masts
Still weary from their struggles with the ocean wave,

While the exotic scent of green tamarind trees,
Which hovers in the air and makes my nostrils flare,
Is blended in my soul with chants of mariners.

De profundis clamavi

J'implore ta pitié, Toi, l'unique que j'aime,
Du fond du gouffre obscur où mon cœur est tombé.
C'est un univers morne à l'horizon plombé,
Où nagent dans la nuit l'horreur et le blasphème.

Un soleil sans chaleur plane au-dessus six mois,
Et les six autres mois la nuit couvre la terre;
C'est un pays plus nu que la terre polaire;
—Ni bêtes, ni ruisseaux, ni verdure, ni bois!

Or il n'est pas d'horreur au monde qui surpasse
La froide cruauté de ce soleil de glace
Et cette immense nuit semblable au vieux Chaos;

Je jalouse le sort des plus vils animaux
Qui peuvent se plonger dans un sommeil stupide,
Tant l'écheveau du temps lentement se dévide!

De profundis clamavi

I beg for thy pity, O Thou, my only love,
From the deep, dark abyss where my heart lies entombed.
It's a bleak, dismal world of horizons lead-gray,
Where horror and blasphemy swirl in the gloom.

A sun without warmth hangs above for six months,
And the other six months darkness blankets the land;
It's a country more stark than the earth at the poles:
—No greenery, no forests, no creatures, no streams!

Now no horror in all the wide world can surpass
The cold, cruel glare of this sun made of ice
And this measureless night like the Chaos of old;

I envy the lot of the meanest of beasts
Who can plunge themselves into the stupor of sleep,
So slowly unravels the long skein of time!

Harmonie du soir

Voici venir les temps où vibrant sur sa tige
Chaque fleur s'évapore ainsi qu'un encensoir;
Les sons et les parfums tournent dans l'air du soir;
Valse mélancolique et langoureux vertige!

Chaque fleur s'évapore ainsi qu'un encensoir;
Le violon frémit comme un cœur qu'on afflige;
Valse mélancolique et langoureux vertige!
Le ciel est triste et beau comme un grand reposoir.

Le violon frémit comme un cœur qu'on afflige,
Un cœur tendre, qui hait le néant vaste et noir!
Le ciel est triste et beau comme un grand reposoir;
Le soleil s'est noyé dans son sang qui se fige.

Un cœur tendre, qui hait le néant vaste et noir,
Du passé lumineux recueille tout vestige!
Le soleil s'est noyé dans son sang qui se fige . . .
Ton souvenir en moi luit comme un ostensoir!

Evening Harmony

And now the time has come when, trembling on its stem,
Each flower, like a censer, into scent dissolves;
Then sounds and perfumes mingle in the evening air;
A melancholy waltz, a languid vertigo!

Each flower, like a censer, into scent dissolves;
The violin laments like an afflicted heart;
A melancholy waltz, a languid vertigo!
The sky is sad and lovely like a *reposoir.**

The violin laments like an afflicted heart,
A tender heart, which hates the vast dark nothingness!
The sky is sad and lovely like a *reposoir.**
The sun has drowned itself in its congealing blood.

A tender heart, which hates the vast dark nothingness,
Will cherish every vestige of the glowing past!
The sun has drowned itself in its congealing blood . . .
Your memory shines within me like an *ostensoir.***

* *reposoir:*   a station or temporary altar, when the Host is carried in
         procession.
** *ostensoir:*   a golden receptacle in which the Host is held.

Le Flacon

Il est de forts parfums pour qui toute matière
Est poreuse. On dirait qu'ils pénètrent le verre.
En ouvrant un coffret venu de l'Orient
Dont la serrure grince et rechigne en criant,

Ou dans une maison déserte quelque armoire
Pleine de l'âcre odeur des temps, poudreuse et noire,
Parfois on trouve un vieux flacon qui se souvient,
D'où jaillit toute vive une âme qui revient.

Mille pensers dormaient, chrysalides funèbres,
Frémissant doucement dans les lourdes ténèbres,
Qui dégagent leur aile et prennent leur essor,
Teintés d'azur, glacés de rose, lamés d'or.

Voilà le souvenir enivrant qui voltige
Dans l'air troublé; les yeux se ferment; le Vertige
Saisit l'âme vaincue et la pousse à deux mains
Vers un gouffre obscurci de miasmes humains;

Il la terrasse au bord d'un gouffre séculaire,
Où, Lazare odorant déchirant son suaire,
Se meut dans son réveil le cadavre spectral
D'un vieil amour ranci, charmant et sépulcral.

Ainsi, quand je serai perdu dans la mémoire
Des hommes, dans le coin d'une sinistre armoire
Quand on m'aura jeté, vieux flacon désolé,
Décrépit, poudreux, sale, abject, visqueux, fêlé,

The Phial

For some potent perfumes, any substance at all
Is porous. It's as if they pass right through the glass.
Upon opening a chest from the far Orient,
Whose hinges and lock creak and groan in protest,

Or some ancient armoire in a vacated house,
Full of time's acrid mustiness, dusty and dark,
One may find an old phial that remembers the past,
Whence emerges, alive, a returning soul's ghost.

Dormant thoughts by the thousand, forlorn chrysalids,
Softly quivering there in the close, humid dark,
Unfold and deploy their sheer wings and take flight,
Tinted azure, glazed roseate, spangled with gold.

Then it's heady remembrance that flutters about
In the unquiet air; the eyes close; Vertigo
Grips the overborne soul and impels with both hands
Toward a chasm by human miasmas obscured;

Knocks it down at the brink of a secular gulf,
Where, a sweet-smelling Lazarus tearing his shroud,
There awakens and stirs the cadaverous ghost
Of an old love turned rancid, sepulchral and suave.

So, when I have been lost in the memory of men,
When off into a corner of some foul armoire
They have cast me, a sorry, decrepit old phial,
Thick with dust, filthy, slimy, repulsive and cracked,

Je serai ton cercueil, aimable pestilence!
Le témoin de ta force et de ta virulence,
Cher poison préparé par les anges! liqueur
Qui me ronge, ô la vie et la mort de mon cœur!

I shall then be thy coffin, beloved pestilence!
The proof of thy potency and virulence,
Thou dear poison prepared by the angels! Liqueur
That destroys me, O life of my heart and its death!

L'Invitation au voyage

Mon enfant, ma soeur,
Songe à la douceur
D'aller là-bas vivre ensemble!
Aimer à loisir,
Aimer et mourir
Au pays qui te ressemble!
Les soleils mouillés
De ces ciels brouillés
Pour mon esprit ont les charmes
Si mystérieux
De tes traîtres yeux,
Brillant à travers leurs larmes.

Là, tout n'est qu'ordre et beauté,
Luxe, calme et volupté.

Des meubles luisants,
Polis par les ans,
Décoreraient notre chambre;
Les plus rares fleurs
Mêlant leurs odeurs
Aux vagues senteurs de l'ambre,
Les riches plafonds,
Les miroirs profonds,
La splendeur orientale,
Tout y parlerait
A l'âme en secret
Sa douce langue natale.

Invitation to the Voyage

Darling, sister mine,
Think how sweet 'twould be
To go live together there!
To love at our ease,
To live, love and die
In that land so like yourself!
The suns blurred by rain
In those cloudy skies
For my spirit have the charms
So mysterious
Of your traitress eyes,
Through their tears shining brightly.

There, all is order, beauty,
Luxury, pleasure and calm.

Gleaming chests and chairs,
Burnished by the years,
Would decorate our chamber;
Rarest flowers in bloom
Blending their perfume
With the faint scent of amber,
Ceilings rich, deep-banked
Mirrors to reflect
Oriental pomp and splendor,
All things there would speak
To the secret soul
In their soft native language.

> Là, tout n'est qu'ordre et beauté,
> Luxe, calme et volupté.

> Vois sur ces canaux
>   Dormir ces vaisseaux
> Dont l'humeur est vagabonde;
>   C'est pour assouvir
>   Ton moindre désir
> Qu'ils viennent du bout du monde.
>   —Les soleils couchants
>   Revêtent les champs,
> Les canaux, la ville entière,
>   D'hyacinthe et d'or;
>   Le monde s'endort
> Dans une chaude lumière.

> Là, tout n'est qu'ordre et beauté,
> Luxe, calme et volupté.

There, all is order, beauty,
Luxury, pleasure and calm.

See on yon canals,
    Sleeping now, those ships
Whose mood is vagabonding.
    'Tis to gratify
    Your slightest desire
That they've come from distant climes.
    —Now the setting sun
    Is clothing the fields
The canals, the town entire,
    In jacinth and gold;
    The world's being lulled
To sleep in a warming light.

There, all is order, beauty,
Luxury, pleasure and calm.

Chant d'automne

I

Bientôt nous plongerons dans les froides ténèbres;
Adieu, vive clarté de nos étés trop courts!
J'entends déjà tomber avec des chocs funèbres
Le bois retentissant sur le pavé des cours.

Tout l'hiver va rentrer dans mon être: colère,
Haine, frissons, horreur, labeur dur et forcé,
Et, comme le soleil dans son enfer polaire,
Mon cœur ne sera plus qu'un bloc rouge et glacé.

J'écoute en frémissant chaque bûche qui tombe;
L'échafaud qu'on bâtit n'a pas d'écho plus sourd.
Mon esprit est pareil à la tour qui succombe
Sous les coups du bélier infatigable et lourd.

Il me semble, bercé par ce choc monotone,
Qu'on cloue en grande hâte un cercueil quelque part . . .
Pour qui? —C'était hier l'été; voici l'automne!
Ce bruit mystérieux sonne comme un départ.

II

J'aime de vos longs yeux la lumière verdâtre,
Douce beauté, mais tout aujourd'hui m'est amer,
Et rien, ni votre amour, ni le boudoir, ni l'âtre,
Ne me vaut le soleil rayonnant sur la mer.

Autumn Song

I

Very soon we'll be plunged into cold, gloomy dark;
O clear light of all-too-brief summer, farewell!
Already I hear the lugubrious thump
Of wood being dropped on courtyard paving-stones.

Once again, all of winter will enter my being:
Anger, hate, disgust, shudders; forced, joyless toil;
And my heart, like the sun in its great polar hell,
Will be naught any more but a frozen red lump.

I listen, and quake at the fall of each log;
No gibbet a-building has an echo more grim;
My spirit succumbs, as the tower to the blows
Of the ponderous, tireless battering-ram.

As I'm lulled by this monotone thudding, it seems
That they're hastily nailing a coffin somewhere . . .
For whom? —In one day, summer's gone, and it's fall!
This strange sound has the ring of a funeral knell.

II

I love the green glint of your long almond eyes,
Beauty sweet, but today for me all is gall,
And no thing—not your love, the boudoir, nor the hearth,
Is to me worth the sun beaming down on the sea.

Et pourtant aimez-moi, tendre cœur! soyez mère
Même pour un ingrat, même pour un méchant;
Amante ou soeur, soyez la douceur éphémère
D'un glorieux automne ou d'un soleil couchant.

Courte tache! La tombe attend; elle est avide!
Ah! laissez-moi, mon front posé sur vos genoux,
Goûter, en regrettant l'été blanc et torride,
De l'arrière-saison le rayon jaune et doux!

Yet love me, tender heart! Be what a mother is
To even a thankless, even a wicked son;
Lover or sister, be the transitory bliss
Of an autumn's glory or a setting sun.

Brief task! for the grave, ever eager, awaits!
So let me, lying here with my head in your lap,
Regretting the torrid white summer, enjoy
The soft golden glow of late autumn's last days!

A une dame créole

Au pays parfumé que le soleil caresse,
J'ai connu, sous un dais d'arbres tout empourprés
Et de palmiers d'où pleut sur les yeux la paresse,
Une dame créole aux charmes ignorés.

Son teint est pâle et chaud; la brune enchanteresse
A dans le cou des airs noblement maniérés;
Grande et svelte en marchant comme une chasseresse,
Son sourire est tranquille et ses yeux assurés.

Si vous alliez, Madame, au vrai pays de gloire,
Sur les bords de la Seine ou de la verte Loire,
Belle digne d'orner les antiques manoirs,

Vous feriez, à l'abri des ombreuses retraites,
Germer mille sonnets dans le cœur des poëtes,
Que vos grands yeux rendraient plus soumis que vos noirs.

To a Creole Lady

In a spice-scented country caressed by the sun,
'Neath an awning of trees all empurpled with bloom
And of palms dripping sloth on the eyes, I once met
A fine Creole lady of singular charms.

Her fair skin's warm of tone; the enchantress brunette
Bears her head with a mannered air, noble and proud;
Tall and svelte, with the stride of a huntress she moves;
Her smile is serene and her glance self-assured.

Should you travel, Milady, to glory's true home
On the banks of the Seine or the emerald Loire,
O beauty to grace any ancient *manoir*,

You would cause, in the shelter of shady retreats,
Many sonnets to sprout in the hearts of our bards,
Whom your great eyes would leave more enslaved
                                        than your blacks.

Tristesses de la lune

Ce soir, la lune rêve avec plus de paresse;
Ainsi qu'une beauté, sur de nombreux coussins,
Qui d'une main distraite et légère caresse
Avant de s'endormir le contour de ses seins,

Sur le dos satiné des molles avalanches,
Mourante, elle se livre aux longues pâmoisons,
Et promène ses yeux sur les visions blanches
Qui montent dans l'azur comme des floraisons.

Quand parfois sur ce globe, en sa langueur oisive,
Elle laisse filer une larme furtive,
Un poëte pieux, ennemi du sommeil,

Dans le creux de sa main prend cette larme pâle,
Aux reflets irisés comme un fragment d'opale,
Et la met dans son cœur loin des yeux du soleil.

Moon-Tears

The moon is most languidly dreaming tonight;
Like a beauty reclining on cushions galore
Who absently, lightly, ere falling asleep,
Caresses the curving contour of her breasts,

Aswoon on the satiny backs of that soft
Avalanche, into somnolent reverie she drifts,
And her eye wanders over the visions of white
Which like clusters of flowers rise into the night.

When sometimes, in her languorous spell, she lets fall
Onto this globe of ours a fugitive tear,
Some poet devout, adversary to sleep,

Will catch in the cup of his hand that pale tear,
Rainbow-hued like a fragment of opal, and hide
It away in his heart from the eye of the sun.

Les Chats

Les amoureux fervents et les savants austères
Aiment également, dans leur mûre saison,
Les chats puissants et doux, orgueil de la maison,
Qui comme eux sont frileux et comme eux sédentaires.

Amis de la science et de la volupté,
Ils cherchent le silence et l'horreur des ténèbres;
L'Erèbe les eût pris pour ses coursiers funèbres,
S'ils pouvaient au servage incliner leur fierté.

Ils prennent en songeant les nobles attitudes
Des grands sphinx allongés au fond des solitudes,
Qui semblent s'endormir dans un rêve sans fin;

Leurs reins féconds sont pleins d'étincelles magiques,
Et des parcelles d'or, ainsi qu'un sable fin,
Etoilent vaguement leurs prunelles mystiques.

Cats

Devout, fervent lovers and scholars austere,
In their ripe season, are equally fond
Of cats, sleek and powerful, pride of the house,
Who like them shun the cold and like them stay at home.

Well-disposed toward knowledge and pleasure, cats
Will seek out the silence and dread of the dark;
Great Erebus' funeral coursers they'd be,
Could they bend their proud spirit to servitude.

They assume, in their musing, the stately pose
Of great sphinxes reclining in vast lonely wastes,
Who seemingly drowse in a dream without end;

Full of magical sparks are their fecund loins,
And flecks of gold, like a fine-sprinkled sand,
Faintly bespangle their mystical eyes.

Les Hiboux

Sous les ifs noirs qui les abritent,
Les hiboux se tiennent rangés,
Ainsi que des dieux étrangers,
Dardant leur œil rouge. Ils méditent.

Sans remuer ils se tiendront
Jusqu'à l'heure mélancolique
Où, poussant le soleil oblique,
Les ténèbres s'établiront.

Leur attitude au sage enseigne
Qu'il faut en ce monde qu'il craigne
Le tumulte et le mouvement;

L'homme ivre d'une ombre qui passe
Porte toujours le châtiment
D'avoir voulu changer de place.

Owls

In the black yews that shelter them,
The owls sit solemn and sedate,
Like alien gods, glaring about
With great red eyes. They meditate.

Quite motionless they will remain
Until the melancholy hour
When, pushing out the slanting sun,
Darkness everywhere will reign.

Their attitude instructs the wise
That in this world one must beware
Of movement, tumult and fanfare;

Whoso will passing shadows chase
The punishment must always bear
For having sought to change his place.

Sépulture

Si par une nuit lourde et sombre
Un bon chrétien, par charité,
Derrière quelque vieux décombre
Enterre votre corps vanté,

A l'heure où les chastes étoiles
Ferment leurs yeux appesantis,
L'araignée y fera ses toiles,
Et la vipère ses petits;

Vous entendrez toute l'année
Sur votre tête condamnée
Les cris lamentables des loups

Et des sorcières faméliques,
Les ébats des vieillards lubriques
Et les complots des noirs filous.

Interment

If on a dark and sultry night
Some good Samaritan inters
Behind some crumbling rubble-heap
That vaunted flesh-and-bone of yours,

When the chaste stars drowsy grow
And close their heavy-lidded eyes,
The spider there will spin her webs
And vipers will beget their young;

Throughout the year you'll surely hear
Above your poor, accursèd head
The lamentable howls of wolves

And shrieks of starveling witches dire,
The sport of lecherous old men
And the foul plots of evil rogues.

Une Gravure fantastique

Ce spectre singulier n'a pour toute toilette,
Grotesquement campé sur son front de squelette,
Qu'un diadème affreux sentant le carnaval.
Sans éperons, sans fouet, il essouffle un cheval,
Fantôme comme lui, rosse apocalyptique,
Qui bave des naseaux comme un épileptique.
Au travers de l'espace ils s'enfoncent tous deux,
Et foulent l'infini d'un sabot hasardeux.
Le cavalier promène un sabre qui flamboie
Sur les foules sans nom que sa monture broie,
Et parcourt, comme un prince inspectant sa maison,
Le cimetière immense et froid, sans horizon,
Où gisent, aux lueurs d'un soleil blanc et terne,
Les peuples de l'histoire ancienne et moderne.

A Fanciful Engraving

This singular specter for sole raiment wears,
Grotesquely clapped onto his skeleton brow,
A ghastly crown smacking of carnival show.
Without whip or spurs, he is winding a horse,
A phantom like him, a nag apocalyptic,
With nostrils afoam like an epileptic.
Through space they go plunging, the two as if one,
And trampling the infinite, reckless of hoof.
The rider is shaking a great flaming sword
At the faceless hosts whom his mount's riding down,
And inspecting on tour, like a prince his domain,
The immense cold necropolis, without horizon,
Where lie dead, in the light of a leaden-white sun,
The peoples of history, ancient and modern.

Le Mort joyeux

Dans une terre grasse et pleine d'escargots
Je veux creuser moi-même une fosse profonde,
Où je puisse à loisir étaler mes vieux os
Et dormir dans l'oubli comme un requin dans l'onde.

Je hais les testaments et je hais les tombeaux;
Plutôt que d'implorer une larme au monde,
Vivant, j'aimerais mieux inviter les corbeaux
A saigner tous les bouts de ma carcasse immonde.

O vers! noirs compagnons sans oreille et sans yeux,
Voyez venir à vous un mort libre et joyeux;
Philosophes viveurs, fils de la pourriture,

A travers ma ruine allez donc sans remords,
Et dites-moi s'il est encor quelque torture
Pour ce vieux corps sans âme et mort parmi les morts.

The Happy Corpse

Somewhere in rich, fertile earth full of snails
I will dig with my own hands a pit wide and deep,
In which I can calmly stretch out my old bones
And sleep in oblivion like a shark in the wave.

No testaments, no mausoleums for me;
Rather than plead with the world for a tear,
I'd prefer, still alive, to beckon the crows
Every inch of my vile, filthy carcass to bleed.

O worms! dark companions with no ear nor eye,
To you now comes a dead man who's happy and free;
Epicurean philosophers, scions of decay,

Feel free then to bore through my ruins at will,
And tell me if some torment still lies in store
For this soulless old body, more dead than alive.

La Cloche Fêlée

Il est amer et doux, pendant les nuits d'hiver,
D'écouter, près du feu qui palpite et qui fume,
Les souvenirs lointains lentement s'élever
Au bruit des carillons qui chantent dans la brume.

Bienheureuse la cloche au gosier vigoureux
Qui, malgré sa vieillesse, alerte et bien portante,
Jette fidèlement son cri religieux,
Ainsi qu'un vieux soldat qui veille sous la tente!

Moi, mon âme est fêlée, et lorsqu'en ses ennuis
Elle veut de ses chants peupler l'air froid des nuits,
Il arrive souvent que sa voix affaiblie

Semble le râle épais d'un blessé qu'on oublie
Au bord d'un lac de sang, sous un grand tas de morts,
Et qui meurt, sans bouger, dans d'immenses efforts.

The Cracked Bell

It is bitter and sweet, during cold winter nights,
To attend, by a fire that crackles and smokes,
As dim, distant memories are slowly called up
By the sound of bell-chimes ringing clear in the fog.

Thrice blessèd the bell with the vigorous throat,
Still spry, sound and healthy in spite of its age,
Which sings out its dutiful paean to God
Like a trusty old soldier on sentinel watch!

As for me, my soul's cracked, and when in its pain
It would people with anthems the night's frosty air,
There often are times when its weakened voice seems

Like the thick mortal gasp of a wounded man left
Near a huge pool of blood, in a great heap of dead,
Who is dying transfixed, every muscle astrain.

Spleen (I)

Pluviôse, irrité contre la ville entière,
De son urne à grands flots verse un froid ténébreux
Aux pâles habitants du voisin cimetière
Et la mortalité sur les faubourgs brumeux.

Mon chat sur le carreau cherchant une litière
Agite sans repos son corps maigre et galeux;
L'âme d'un vieux poëte erre dans la gouttière
Avec la triste voix d'un fantôme frileux.

Le bourdon se lamente, et la bûche enfumée
Accompagne en fausset la pendule enrhumée,
Cependant qu'en un jeu plein de sales parfums,

Héritage fatal d'une vieille hydropique,
Le beau valet de cœur et la dame de pique
Causent sinistrement de leurs amours défunts.

Late January

Pluviôse,* sorely vexed with the town as a whole,
From his urn pours out copious drafts of dark cold
For the neighboring churchyard's inhabitants pale
And mortality over the foggy faubourgs.

My cat, gaunt and mangy, keeps circling about,
Trying vainly to find a soft bed on the tile;
An old poet's soul prowls the rainspout and wails
With the querulous voice of a shivering wraith.

The great bell laments, and the smoky log whines
Obbligato falsetto to the clock's rheumy wheeze,
While in a deck of cards that reeks of cheap perfumes,

Some dropsical old woman's mortal legacy,
The handsome knave of hearts and the queen of spades
Chat surreptitiously of their defunct amours.

* Pluviôse: a winter month of France's short-lived Revolutionary calendar.

Spleen (II)

J'ai plus de souvenirs que si j'avais mille ans.

Un gros meuble à tiroirs encombrés de bilans,
De vers, de billets doux, de procès, de romances,
Avec de lourds cheveux roulés dans des quittances,
Cache moins de secrets que mon triste cerveau.
C'est une pyramide, un immense caveau,
Qui contient plus de morts que la fosse commune.

—Je suis un cimetière abhorré de la lune,
Où comme des remords, se traînent de longs vers
Qui s'acharnent toujours sur mes morts les plus chers.
Je suis un vieux boudoir plein de roses fanées,
Où gît tout un fouillis de modes surannées,
Où les pastels plaintifs et les pâles Boucher,
Seuls, respirent l'odeur d'un flacon débouché.

Rien n'égale en longueur les boiteuses journées,
Quand, sous les lourds flocons des neigeuses années,
L'ennui, fruit de la morne incuriosité,
Prend les proportions de l'immortalité.
—Désormais tu n'es plus, ô matière vivante!
Qu'un granit entouré d'une vague épouvante,
Assoupi dans le fond d'un Sahara brumeux;
Un vieux sphinx ignoré du monde insoucieux,
Oublié sur la carte, et dont l'humeur farouche
Ne chante qu'aux rayons du soleil qui se couche!

The Sphinx

I've more memories than were I a thousand years old.

A great chest of drawers, crammed full of accounts,
Of verses, love-letters, law-papers, songs,
With thick locks of hair rolled up in receipts,
Hides away fewer secrets than my wretched brain.
It's a pyramid, a catacomb vaulted and vast,
Wherein corpses lie thicker than in potter's field.

—I am a cemetery shunned by the moon,
Where like pangs of remorse, long worms crawl about,
Ever eating away at my most cherished dead.
I'm a fusty boudoir full of roses all sere,
Where lies strewn a great jumble of outmoded gowns,
Where pale Boucher portraits and plaintive pastels
Breathe lonely the scent from an unstoppered vial.

There is nothing so long as the slow-limping days,
Those ponderous snowflakes that drift into years,
When ennui, the offspring of glum apathy,
Takes on the dimensions of immortality.
—O live flesh and blood! thou art henceforth no more
Than an outcrop of granite beset by vague terror,
Languishing deep in some hazy Sahara;
An old sphinx unmarked by the indifferent world,
Unmapped and forgotten, whose peevishness sings
To none save the rays of the westering sun!

Spleen (III)

Je suis comme le roi d'un pays pluvieux,
Riche, mais impuissant, jeune et pourtant très-vieux,
Qui, de ses précepteurs méprisant les courbettes,
S'ennuie avec ses chiens comme avec d'autres bêtes.
Rien ne peut l'égayer, ni gibier, ni faucon,
Ni son peuple mourant en face du balcon.
Du bouffon favori la grotesque ballade
Ne distrait plus le front de ce cruel malade;
Son lit fleurdelisé se transforme en tombeau,
Et les dames d'atour, pour qui tout prince est beau,
Ne savent plus trouver l'impudique toilette
Pour tirer un souris de ce jeune squelette.
Le savant qui lui fait de l'or n'a jamais pu
De son être extirper l'élément corrompu,
Et dans ces bains de sang qui des Romains nous viennent
Et dont sur leurs vieux jours les puissants se souviennent,
Il n'a su réchauffer ce cadavre hébété
Où coule au lieu de sang l'eau verte du Léthé.

Tædium vitæ

I am like the king of some pluvious land,
Wealthy, but impotent, young and yet decrepit,
Who scorns his preceptors' obsequious bows
And is bored with his dogs as with other dumb brutes.
Nothing can cheer him—not hunting, nor falconry,
Nor his people groveling before the balcony.
The grotesque ballade of his favorite buffoon
No longer amuses this sick, cruel man;
His fleur-de-lys bed has turned into a bier,
And the ladies at court, who deem any prince fair,
No longer can find the provocative gown
To elicit a smile from this young skeleton.
The sage who makes gold for him hasn't known how
To distill the base element out of his soul;
And in blood-baths, for which we've the Romans to thank,
And which despots remember when feeling their age,
He has failed to warm up that benumbed, lifeless corpse
Through which flows not blood, but Lethe's green flood.

Spleen (IV)

Quand le ciel bas et lourd pèse comme un couvercle
Sur l'esprit gémissant en proie aux longs ennuis,
Et que de l'horizon embrassant tout le cercle
Il nous verse un jour noir plus triste que les nuits;

Quand la terre est changée en un cachot humide,
Où l'Espérance, comme une chauve-souris,
S'en va battant les murs de son aile timide
Et se cognant la tête à des plafonds pourris;

Quand la pluie étalant ses immenses traînées,
D'une vaste prison imite les barreaux,
Et qu'un peuple muet d'infâmes araignées
Vient tendre ses filets au fond de nos cerveaux,

Des cloches tout à coup sautent avec furie
Et lancent vers le ciel un affreux hurlement,
Ainsi que des esprits errants et sans patrie
Qui se mettent à geindre opiniâtrément.

—Et de longs corbillards, sans tambours ni musique,
Défilent lentement dans mon âme; l'Espoir,
Vaincu, pleure, et l'Angoisse atroce, despotique,
Sur mon crâne incliné plante son drapeau noir.

Despair

When the low, leaden sky presses down like a lid
On the suffering spirit in endless travail,
And when from around the horizon's whole rim
It pours us dark daylight more somber than night;

When the earth is turned into a dank dungeon cell
Wherein Hope, like a fluttering bat in the gloom,
In vain beats the walls with a timorous wing
And bruises her head on the ceiling's foul slime;

When rain, hanging out its immense sweeping trains,
Resembles a vast, murky prison's thick bars,
And a host of vile spiders soundlessly come
To spin their damp webs in the depths of our brains,

Then bells, of a sudden, explode in a rage
And fling toward the heavens a dolorous cry,
Like wandering spirits in search of a home,
Beginning an obstinate, whimpering plaint.

—And in silent cortège, without music or drums,
Long black hearses dead-slowly defile in my soul;
Hope, vanquished, weeps; and fierce Anguish, despotic,
Upon my bowed skull firmly plants her black flag.

Obsession

Grands bois, vous m'effrayez comme des cathédrales;
Vous hurlez comme l'orgue; et dans nos cœurs maudits,
Chambres d'éternel deuil où vibrent de vieux râles,
Répondent les échos de vos *De profundis*.

Je te hais, Océan! tes bonds et tes tumultes,
Mon esprit les retrouve en lui; ce rire amer
De l'homme vaincu, plein de sanglots et d'insultes,
Je l'entends dans le rire énorme de la mer.

Comme tu me plairais, ô nuit! sans ces étoiles
Dont la lumière parle un langage connu!
Car je cherche le vide, et le noir, et le nu!

Mais les ténèbres sont elles-mêmes des toiles
Où vivent, jaillissant de mon œil par milliers,
Des êtres disparus aux regards familiers.

Obsession

Great forests, you daunt me as cathedrals do;
You shout like the organ; and in our stricken hearts,
Mourning-chambers where ceaselessly quaver old rales,
The echoes of your *De profundis* resound.

Vast Ocean, I hate you! Your turmoil and heave
My spirit within itself finds; that bitter laugh
Of the defeated man, fraught with sobs and affronts,
I can hear in the monstrous guffaw of the sea.

How you'd please me, O Night, were it not for those stars,
Whose light speaks a language I know! For I seek
Nothing more than the void, and the featureless dark!

But the darkness itself is a canvas whereon,
Erupting by thousands from out of my eye,
Spring to life recognizable, long-vanished souls.

Le Goût du néant

Morne esprit, autrefois amoureux de la lutte,
L'Espoir, dont l'éperon attisait ton ardeur,
Ne veut plus t'enfourcher! Couche-toi sans pudeur,
Vieux cheval dont le pied à chaque obstacle bute.

Résigne-toi, mon cœur; dors ton sommeil de brute.

Esprit vaincu, fourbu! Pour toi, vieux maraudeur,
L'amour n'a plus de goût, non plus que la dispute;
Adieu donc, chants du cuivre et soupirs de la flûte!
Plaisirs, ne tentez plus un cœur sombre et boudeur!

Le Printemps adorable a perdu son odeur!

Et le Temps m'engloutit minute par minute,
Comme la neige immense un corps pris de roideur;
Je contemple d'en haut le globe en sa rondeur
Et je n'y cherche plus l'abri d'une cahute.

Avalanche, veux-tu m'emporter dans ta chute?

Taste for Oblivion

Wretched spirit, once eager the battle to join,
Thy old rider Hope, whose spur fanned thy flame,
Will no longer mount thee! Lie down without shame,
Old war-horse who stumbles at every loose stone.

Resign thyself, heart; sleep thy dumb-brutish sleep.

Broken-down, foundered spirit! Old charger, for thee
There's no savor in love any more, nor dispute;
So farewell, singing brass and soft, sighing flute!
Delights, tempt no more a morose, sullen heart!

The adored goddess Springtime her fragrance has lost!

And minute by minute I'm swallowed by Time,
As a stiffening corpse is engulfed by vast snow;
I behold from aloft the whole round of the globe
And I no longer look for a sheltering wall.

Avalanche, wilt thou sweep me away in thy fall?

L'Héautontimorouménos

Je te frapperai sans colère
Et sans haine, comme un boucher,
Comme Moïse le rocher!
Et je ferai de ta paupière,

Pour abreuver mon Saharah,
Jaillir les eaux de la souffrance.
Mon désir gonflé d'espérance
Sur tes pleurs salés nagera

Comme un vaisseau qui prend le large,
Et dans mon cœur qu'ils soûleront
Tes chers sanglots retentiront
Comme un tambour qui bat la charge!

Ne suis-je pas un faux accord
Dans la divine symphonie,
Grâce à la vorace Ironie
Qui me secoue et qui me mord?

Elle est dans ma voix, la criarde!
C'est tout mon sang, ce poison noir!
Je suis le sinistre miroir
Où la mégère se regarde!

Je suis la plaie et le couteau!
Je suis le soufflet et la joue!
Je suis les membres et la roue,
Et la victime et le bourreau!

The Self-Tormentor

I'll strike you coldly, without hate
Or anger, as a butcher strikes,
As Moses smote the Horeb rock!
And from your lids I'll make gush forth,

To irrigate my Sahará,
The floods of suffering and pain.
My hot desire, blown large by hope,
Will swim upon your salt tears like

A ship that's putting out to sea,
And in my heart, made drunk thereby,
Your cherished sobs will echo like
A drum that's beating out the charge!

Am I not a discordant note
In God's celestial symphony,
Thanks to voracious Irony
Who bites and shakes me in her jaws?

She's in my voice, the strident scold!
It's all my blood, this poison black!
I am the mirror sinister
Wherein the shrew regards herself!

I am the stab-wound and the knife!
I am the stung cheek and the slap!
I am the members and the wheel,
The victim and the hangman too!

Je suis de mon cœur le vampire,
—Un de ces grands abandonnés
Au rire éternel condamnés,
Et qui ne peuvent plus sourire!

I am the vampire of my heart,
—One of those great forsaken few
Condemned eternally to laugh,
And able nevermore to smile!

L'Horloge

Horloge! dieu sinistre, effrayant, impassible,
Dont le doigt nous menace et nous dit: "Souviens-toi!"
Les vibrantes Douleurs dans ton cœur plein d'effroi
Se planteront bientôt comme dans une cible;

Le Plaisir vaporeux fuira vers l'horizon
Ainsi qu'une sylphide au fond de la coulisse;
Chaque instant te dévore un morceau du délice
A chaque homme accordé pour toute sa saison.

Trois mille six cents fois par heure, la Seconde
Chuchote: *Souviens-toi!* —Rapide, avec sa voix
D'insecte, Maintenant dit: Je suis Autrefois,
Et j'ai pompé ta vie avec ma trompe immonde!

Remember! Souviens-toi! prodigue! *Esto memor!*
(Mon gosier de métal parle toutes les langues!)
Les minutes, mortel folâtre, sont des gangues
Qu'il ne faut pas lâcher sans en extraire l'or!

Souviens-toi que le Temps est un joueur avide
Qui gagne sans tricher, à tout coup! c'est la loi.
Le jour décroît; la nuit augmente; *souviens-toi!*
Le gouffre a toujours soif; la clepsydre se vide.

Tantôt sonnera l'heure où le divin Hasard,
Où l'auguste Vertu, ton épouse encor vierge,
Où le Repentir même (oh! la dernière auberge!)
Où tout te dira: "Meurs, vieux lâche! il est trop tard!"

The Clock

O Clock! thou impassive, dread, sinister god,
Whose menacing finger "Remember!" exhorts,
The shattering Griefs that thy fearsome heart holds
Will soon, like winged shafts in a target, strike home!

Ephemeral Pleasure will fade from the scene
As a sylphid flees offstage and into the wings;
Each moment devours one more portion of those
Sweet delights meted out for his lifetime to each.

Three thousand six hundred times every hour,
The Second still whispers: "Remember!" Swift Now,
With its insect-like voice, ticks out: "I am the Past,
And my filthy proboscis has sucked out thy life!"

Souviens-toi! Remember! Wastrel! *Esto memor!*
(My gullet of metal speaks all the world's tongues!)
Feckless mortal, the minutes are matrices, gangues,
Which must not be let go without yielding their gold!

Remember that Time is a dice-player keen
Who wins without fraud, every cast! That's the law.
The day wanes; the night waxes; *remember!* The pit
Is forever athirst, and the clepsydra drains.

The hour will soon strike when omnipotent Chance,
When radiant Virtue, thy still-virgin spouse,
When Repentance itself (ah—the last wayside inn!),
When all will say: "Die, old poltroon! It's too late!"

from the cycle
"Tableaux parisiens"

Paysage

Je veux, pour composer chastement mes églogues,
Coucher auprès du ciel, comme les astrologues,
Et, voisin des clochers, écouter en rêvant
Leurs hymnes solennels emportés par le vent.
Les deux mains au menton, du haut de ma mansarde,
Je verrai l'atelier qui chante et qui bavarde;
Les tuyaux, les clochers, ces mâts de la cité,
Et les grands ciels qui font rêver d'éternité.

Il est doux, à travers les brumes, de voir naître
L'étoile dans l'azur, la lampe à la fenêtre,
Les fleuves de charbon monter au firmament
Et la lune verser son pâle enchantement.

Je verrai les printemps, les étés, les automnes;
Et quand viendra l'hiver aux neiges monotones,
Je fermerai partout portières et volets
Pour bâtir dans la nuit mes féeriques palais.
Alors je rêverai des horizons bleuâtres,
Des jardins, des jets d'eau pleurant dans les albâtres,
Des baisers, des oiseaux chantant soir et matin,
Et tout ce que l'Idylle a de plus enfantin.
L'Emeute, tempêtant vainement à ma vitre,
Ne fera pas lever mon front de mon pupitre;
Car je serai plongé dans cette volupté,
D'évoquer le Printemps avec ma volonté,
De tirer un soleil de mon cœur, et de faire
De mes pensers brûlants une tiède atmosphère.

Landscape

I want, in which chastely my eclogues to pen,
A room near the sky, such as star-gazers have,
Where I'll listen and dream as my neighbors, the bells,
Waft forth on the wind their devout, solemn hymns.
Gazing out, chin in hands, from my garret on high,
I'll see ateliers humming with chatter and song;
Smoke-stacks and church-spires, the city's tall masts,
And the heavens evoking eternity's dreams.

It is lovely to watch, through the haze, as each star
Is born in the blue, in each window a lamp;
As the rivers of soot to the firmament rise,
And the moon's pale enchantment is cast over all.

I shall see springtimes, and summers, and falls,
And when winter sets in with its tedious snows,
I shall close all door-curtains and shutters, and then
I shall build in the night fairy castles in Spain.
I shall dream then of distant horizons blue-grey,
Of gardens, of white marble fountains that weep.
Of kisses, of birds singing morning and eve,
And of all that's most childlike in Idyll's romance.
Though Riot be raging outside in the street,
I shall not even lift up my head from my desk;
For I'll be enrapt in the utter delight
Of conjuring Spring by the strength of my will,
Extracting a sun from my heart, and with thoughts
That burn hotly, creating a warm atmosphere.

Le Soleil

Le long du vieux faubourg, où pendent aux masures
Les persiennes, abri des secrètes luxures,
Quand le soleil cruel frappe à traits redoublés
Sur la ville et les champs, sur les toits et les blés,
Je vais m'exercer seul à ma fantasque escrime,
Flairant dans tous les coins les hasards de la rime,
Trébuchant sur les mots comme sur les pavés,
Heurtant parfois des vers depuis longtemps rêvés.

Ce père nourricier, ennemi des chloroses,
Eveille dans les champs les vers comme les roses;
Il fait s'évaporer les soucis vers le ciel,
Et remplit les cerveaux et les ruches de miel.
C'est lui qui rajeunit les porteurs de béquilles
Et les rend gais et doux comme des jeunes filles,
Et commande aux moissons de croître et de mûrir
Dans le cœur immortel qui toujours veut fleurir!

Quand, ainsi qu'un poète, il descend dans les villes,
Il ennoblit le sort des choses les plus viles,
Et s'introduit en roi, sans bruit et sans valets,
Dans tous les hôpitaux et dans tous les palais.

The Sun

Through the old part of town, where on cottages hang
Heavy shutters, a screen for clandestine debauch,
When the sun beats down fiercely with supercharged rays
Upon city and countryside, rooftops and crops,
I go poetry-fencing, my own fancy's game,
In all corners *en garde* against dangers of rhyme,
Stumbling over words as on loose paving-stones,
And sometimes upon lines heard long since in my dreams.

That benign foster-father, chloroses' great foe,
Wakens verses, like roses, from sleep in the fields;
He evaporates cares, turns them into thin air;
He fills bee-hives with honey and brains with ideas.
It is he who restores to crutch-bearers their youth
And makes them as gentle and gay as young girls.
He commands all the crops to grow tall and mature
In their immortal hearts, which would rather just bloom!

When he comes, like a poet, down into a town,
He ennobles the fate of the lowliest things,
And like a good king, without suite or fanfare,
Penetrates every poorhouse and every chateau.

Les Sept Vieillards

Fourmillante cité, cité pleine de rêves,
Où le spectre, en plein jour, raccroche le passant!
Les mystères partout coulent comme des sèves
Dans les canaux étroits du colosse puissant.

Un matin, cependant que dans la triste rue
Les maisons, dont la brume allongeait la hauteur,
Simulaient les deux quais d'une rivière accrue,
Et que, décor semblable à l'âme de l'acteur,

Un brouillard sale et jaune inondait tout l'espace,
Je suivais, roidissant mes nerfs comme un héros
Et discutant avec mon âme déjà lasse,
Le faubourg secoué par les lourds tombereaux.

Tout à coup, un vieillard dont les guenilles jaunes
Imitaient la couleur de ce ciel pluvieux,
Et dont l'aspect aurait fait pleuvoir les aumônes,
Sans la méchanceté qui luisait dans ses yeux,

M'apparut. On eût dit sa prunelle trempée
Dans le fiel; son regard aiguisait les frimas,
Et sa barbe à longs poils, roide comme une épée,
Se projetait, pareille à celle de Judas.

Il n'était pas voûté, mais cassé, son échine
Faisant avec sa jambe un parfait angle droit,
Si bien que son bâton, parachevant sa mine,
Lui donnait la tournure et le pas maladroit

The Seven Old Men

City teeming with life, city pregnant with dreams,
Where ghosts, in broad daylight, accost passers-by!
Eerie mysteries flow like tree-sap everywhere
Through the mighty colossus's strait passageways.

One morning, when buildings on drab, dismal streets,
Looming taller by half in the mist-laden air,
Simulated the banks of a river in flood,
And when, a décor like the thespian's soul,

An unclean yellow fog inundated all space,
I was walking, rehearsing my soul's weary woes,
And heroically steeling my nerves to the noise
And vibration of garbage-carts rumbling by.

Suddenly an old man, clad in yellowish rags
Imitating the hue of that pluvious sky,
And whose looks would have earned him a shower of alms
Had there not been a venomous glint in his eye,

Stood before me. His eyes, you'd have said, were adrip
With malice: their glance put an edge on the cold;
And his whiskers, long-haired and as stiff as a sword,
Jutted out from his face, like foul Judas's beard.

He was not merely bent, but quite broken: his spine
With his leg made a perfect right angle, and this,
With his stick to top off the effect of his mien,
Made him look as ungainly of figure and gait

D'un quadrupède infirme ou d'un juif à trois pattes.
Dans la neige et la boue il allait s'empêtrant,
Comme s'il écrasait des morts sous ses savates,
Hostile à l'univers plutôt qu'indifférent.

Son pareil le suivait: barbe, œil, dos, bâton, loques,
Nul trait ne distinguait, du même enfer venu,
Ce jumeau centenaire, et ces spectres baroques
Marchaient du même pas vers un but inconnu.

A quel complot infâme étais-je donc en butte,
Ou quel méchant hasard ainsi m'humiliait?
Car je comptai sept fois, de minute en minute,
Ce sinistre vieillard qui se multipliait!

Que celui-là qui rit de mon inquiétude,
Et qui n'est pas saisi d'un frisson fraternel,
Songe bien que malgré tant de décrepitude
Ces sept monstres hideux avaient l'air éternel!

Aurais-je, sans mourir, contemplé le huitième,
Sosie inexorable, ironique et fatal,
Dégoûtant Phénix, fils et père de lui-même?
—Mais je tournai le dos au cortège infernal.

Exaspéré comme un ivrogne qui voit double,
Je rentrai, je fermai ma porte, épouvanté,
Malade et morfondu, l'esprit fiévreux et trouble,
Blessé par le mystère et par l'absurdité!

Vainement ma raison voulait prendre la barre;
La tempête en jouant déroutait ses efforts,
Et mon âme dansait, dansait, vieille gabarre
Sans mâts, sur une mer monstrueuse et sans bords!

As a lame quadruped or a three-legged Jew.
He went slogging along in the snow and the mud
As if trampling dead bodies beneath his old shoes—
To the universe hostile, not indifferent.

After him came his double: beard, eye, back, stick, rags—
Not a single trait differed in this perfect twin
Centenarian from the same hell, and in step
These weird specters marched off, destination unknown.

By what infamous plot was I victimized here,
Or by what foul mischance to such horror exposed?
For I counted, from minute to minute, five more,
As that sinister oldster was cloned sevenfold!

Let whoso is amused at my anxiety
And not seized with a brotherly shudder, take note
That these hideous monsters, all seven, despite
Their decrepitude, looked quite immortal to me!

Could I have survived, had I sighted an eighth—
Implacable Sosia, ironic, *fatal,*
Or revolting Phœníx, his own father and son?
But I turned my back on the infernal cortège.

Mortified as a drunk seeing double, I fled
Back behind my locked door, terror-stricken, aghast,
Feeling nauseous, feverish, chilled to the bone,
My mind wounded, undone by enigma and farce.

In vain did my reason try taking the helm;
The storm raging on caused its efforts to fail,
And my soul, an old barge without masts, helplessly
Pitched and tossed on a monstrous and limitless sea!

Les Aveugles

Contemple-les, mon âme; ils sont vraiment affreux!
Pareils aux mannequins; vaguement ridicules;
Terribles, singuliers comme les somnambules;
Dardant on ne sait où leurs globes ténébreux.

Leurs yeux, d'où la divine étincelle est partie,
Comme s'ils regardaient au loin, restent levés
Au ciel; on ne les voit jamais vers les pavés
Pencher rêveusement leur tête appesantie.

Ils traversent ainsi le noir illimité,
Ce frère du silence éternel. O cité!
Pendant qu'autour de nous tu chantes, ris et beugles,

Eprise du plaisir jusqu'à l'atrocité,
Vois! je me traîne aussi! mais, plus qu'eux hébété,
Je dis: Que cherchent-ils au Ciel, tous ces aveugles?

The Blind

Behold them, my soul; how ghastly they are!
Like mannequins, vaguely ridiculous, stiff;
Like sleep-walkers, frightening, eerie, bizarre;
Rolling their sightless orbs this way and that.

Their eyes, from which the divine spark is fled,
As if gazing afar, remain raised to the sky;
You never see one of them hanging his head
Heavily, musingly down toward the street.

They traverse in this fashion the limitless dark,
That twin of eternal silence. O city!
While you all around us laugh, bellow and sing,

So madly enamored of pleasure—look here!
I too shuffle along! But bemused more than they,
I say: What seek they in Heaven, all these blind?

Une Passante

La rue assourdissante autour de moi hurlait.
Longue, mince, en grand deuil, douleur majestueuse,
Une femme passa, d'une main fastueuse
Soulevant, balançant le feston et l'ourlet;

Agile et noble, avec sa jambe de statue.
Moi, je buvais, crispé comme un extravagant,
Dans son œil, ciel livide où germe l'ouragan,
La douceur qui fascine et le plaisir qui tue.

Un éclair . . . puis la nuit! —Fugitive beauté
Dont le regard m'a fait soudainement renaître,
Ne te verrai-je plus que dans l'éternité?

Ailleurs, bien loin d'ici! trop tard! *jamais* peut-être!
Car j'ignore où tu fuis, tu ne sais où je vais,
O toi que j'eusse aimée, ô toi qui le savais!

A Woman Passing By

All around roared the deafening din of the street.
Tall, slim, in deep mourning, majestic in grief,
A woman walked by, with one sumptuous hand
Uplifting and swinging festoon and stitched hem;

Light-footed, patrician, of statuesque limb.
As for me, mouth agape like a fool, I drank in
From her eyes, livid sky where the hurricane brews,
The sweetness that charms and the pleasure that kills.

One bolt—then the dark! Evanescent beauty
At whose glance I was suddenly born anew,
Shall I see you no more save in some after-life?

Far away! Or too late! Or perhaps *nevermore*!
For I know not where you flee, nor you where I go,
O you I would have loved, you who knew it was so!

Le Crépuscule du soir

Voici le soir charmant, ami du criminel;
Il vient comme un complice, à pas de loup; le ciel
Se ferme lentement comme une grande alcôve,
Et l'homme impatient se change en bête fauve.

O soir, aimable soir, désiré par celui
Dont les bras, sans mentir, peuvent dire: Aujourd'hui
Nous avons travaillé! —C'est le soir qui soulage
Les esprits que dévore une douleur sauvage,
Le savant obstiné dont le front s'alourdit,
Et l'ouvrier courbé qui regagne son lit.
Cependant des démons malsains dans l'atmosphère
S'éveillent lourdement, comme des gens d'affaire,
Et cognent en volant les volets et l'auvent.
A travers les lueurs que tourmente le vent
La prostitution s'allume dans les rues;
Comme une fourmilière elle ouvre ses issues;
Partout elle se fraye un occulte chemin,
Ainsi que l'ennemi qui tente un coup de main;
Elle remue au sein de la cité de fange
Comme un ver qui dérobe à l'Homme ce qu'il mange.
On entend çà et là les cuisines siffler,
Les théâtres glapir, les orchestres ronfler;
Les tables d'hôte, dont le jeu fait les délices,
S'emplissent de catins et d'escrocs, leurs complices,
Et les voleurs, qui n'ont ni trêve ni merci,
Vont bientôt commencer leur travail, eux aussi,
Et forcer doucement les portes et les caisses
Pour vivre quelques jours et vêtir leurs maîtresses.

Nightfall

Now here's charming evening, the criminal's friend;
Stealthily, like an accomplice, it comes;
The skies slowly close like a great alcove-bed,
And man just can't wait to become a wild beast.

O evening, dear evening, so longed for by him
Whose two arms can truthfully say, "Today
We have labored!" —It's evening that brings sweet relief
To spirits devoured by a desperate grief,
To the painstaking scholar with dull, aching brow
And the bone-weary worker regaining his bed.
But meanwhile, foul demons abroad in the air
Awaken lethargic, like men of affairs,
And fly about banging on shutters and eaves.
As the wind swoops down on the darkening streets,
Prostitution lights up with its lurid gleams;
Like an anthill it opens its outlet holes;
It makes its way secretly everywhere,
Like the enemy massing to mount an attack;
It stirs in the bowels of the precincts of vice
Like a tapeworm usurping the food humans eat.
Here and there one hears kitchens sizzle and hiss,
Theaters yammer and orchestras blare;
Supper clubs, where it's gambling that's all the rage,
Are filling with bawds and their allies, the crooks;
And ubiquitous burglars, who never call truce,
They likewise will shortly be setting to work,
Surreptitiously jimmying doors and tills
To subsist a few days and to dress up their jills.

Recueille-toi, mon âme, en ce grave moment,
Et ferme ton oreille à ce rugissement.
C'est l'heure où les douleurs des malades s'aigrissent!
La sombre Nuit les prend à la gorge; ils finissent
Leur destinée et vont vers le gouffre commun;
L'hôpital se remplit de leurs soupirs. —Plus d'un
Ne viendra plus chercher la soupe parfumée,
Au coin du feu, le soir, auprès d'une âme aimée.

Encore la plupart n'ont-ils jamais connu
La douceur du foyer et n'ont jamais vécu!

Reflect, O my soul, at this fateful hour,
And turn a deaf ear to its racketing roar.
It's the time when the pains of the stricken grow sharp!
Somber Night grips them now by the throat; they live out
Their span and draw near to the common abyss;
The hospital's filled with their sighs. —More than one
Will come never again to share savory soup
By the fire, in the evening, with some beloved soul.

Why, most of them never even have known
The sweetness of home, and have never lived!

L'Amour du mensonge

Quand je te vois passer, ô ma chère indolente,
Au chant des instruments qui se brise au plafond
Suspendant ton allure harmonieuse et lente,
Et promenant l'ennui de ton regard profond;

Quand je contemple, aux feux du gaz qui le colore,
Ton front pâle, embelli par un morbide attrait,
Où les torches du soir allument une aurore,
Et tes yeux attirants comme ceux d'un portrait,

Je me dis: Qu'elle est belle! et bizarrement fraîche!
Le souvenir massif, royale et lourde tour,
La couronne, et son cœur, meurtri comme une pêche,
Est mûr, comme son corps, pour le savant amour.

Es-tu le fruit d'automne aux saveurs souveraines?
Es-tu vase funèbre attendant quelques pleurs,
Parfum qui fait rêver aux oasis lointaines,
Oreiller caressant, ou corbeille de fleurs?

Je sais qu'il est des yeux, des plus mélancoliques,
Qui ne recèlent point de secrets précieux;
Beaux écrins sans joyaux, médaillons sans reliques,
Plus vides, plus profonds que vous-mêmes, ô Cieux!

Mais ne suffit-il pas que tu sois l'apparence,
Pour réjouir un cœur qui fuit la vérité?
Qu'importe ta bêtise ou ton indifférence?
Masque ou décor, salut! J'adore ta beauté.

Love of the Lie

When I see you pass by, my dear indolent one,
As the music breaks up on the ceiling above
Suspending your slow, graceful movement, and then
Glancing 'round with that look of profoundest ennui;

When I contemplate, tinted with lights by the gas,
Your pale forehead, embellished by one beauty-spot,
Where the torches of evening are kindling a dawn,
And your eyes which like those of a portrait compel,

I think: How lovely she is! How strangely cool!
She is memory massive, a great royal tower,
The crown; and her heart, soft and bruised like a peach,
Is ripe, like her body, for sweet, knowing love.

Are you autumn's late fruit with its flavors supreme?
A funeral vase that's awaiting some tears?
A perfume that stirs dreams of oases remote,
A pillow's caress, or a basket of flowers?

I know there are eyes, of the most melancholy,
Which not even one precious secret conceal:
Jewel-cases sans gems, reliquaries sans bones,
More empty and deeper, O heavens, than yourselves!

But is outward appearance not all you need be
To bring joy to a heart that recoils from the truth?
So you're stupid, indifferent—what's that to me?
Mask or décor, all hail! I adore your beauty.

La servante au grand cœur dont vous étiez jalouse,
Et qui dort son sommeil sous une humble pelouse,
Nous devrions pourtant lui porter quelques fleurs.
Les morts, les pauvres morts, ont de grandes douleurs,
Et quand octobre souffle, émondeur des vieux arbres,
Son vent mélancolique à l'entour de leurs marbres,
Certe, ils doivent trouver les vivants bien ingrats,
A dormir, comme ils font, chaudement dans leurs draps,
Tandis que, dévorés de noires songeries,
Sans compagnon de lit, sans bonnes causeries,
Vieux squelettes gelés travaillés par le ver,
Ils sentent s'égoutter les neiges de l'hiver
Et le siècle couler, sans qu'amis ni famille
Remplacent les lambeaux qui pendent à leur grille.

Lorsque la bûche siffle et chante, si le soir,
Calme, dans le fauteuil, je la voyais s'asseoir,
Si, par une nuit bleue et froide de décembre,
Je la trouvais tapie en un coin de ma chambre,
Grave, et venant du fond de son lit éternel
Couver l'enfant grandi de son œil maternel,
Que pourrais-je répondre à cette âme pieuse,
Voyant tomber des pleurs de sa paupière creuse?

The Nanny

The great-hearted nanny whom you were jealous of ,
And who now sleeps beneath a humble patch of sod—
We really ought to take her flowers now and then.
The dead, poor things, have sorrows infinite to bear,
And when October, pruner of old trees, blows in
With mournful wind that moans around their marble stones,
They surely must find us, the living, ingrates all,
To sleep so snug and warm beneath our coverlets,
While they, the dead, consumed by bitter reveries,
With none to share their bed, with no good pillow-talk,
Outworn and frozen skeletons prey to the worm,
Are feeling winter snowfalls melt and drain away,
And seeing ages pass, while no kinfolk nor friends
Come to replace the tattered wreaths hung on their grilles.

If, when at dusk the fire-log sings and whines, I were
To see her sitting quietly in the big chair;
If, on some frosty blue December night, I were
To find her huddled in a corner of my room,
Concerned, and coming from her deep eternal bed
To keep maternal watch over the grown-up child,
What could I find to say to that dear pious soul
On seeing teardrops falling from her sunken lids?

Brumes et pluies

O fins d'automne, hivers, printemps trempés de boue,
Endormeuses saisons! je vous aime et vous loue
D'envelopper ainsi mon cœur et mon cerveau
D'un linceul vaporeux et d'un vague tombeau.

Dans cette grande plaine où l'autan froid se joue,
Où par les longues nuits la girouette s'enroue,
Mon âme mieux qu'au temps du tiède renouveau
Ouvrira largement ses ailes de corbeau.

Rien n'est plus doux au cœur plein de choses funèbres,
Et sur qui dès longtemps descendent les frimas,
O blafardes saisons, reines de nos climats,

Que l'aspect permanent de vos pâles ténèbres,
—Si ce n'est, par un soir sans lune, deux à deux,
D'endormir la douleur sur un lit hasardeux.

Fogs and Rains

O late autumns, winters, mud-steeped early springs,
Soporiferous seasons! I love and praise you
For enwrapping my heart and my brain as you do
In a vaporous shroud and a kind of gray tomb.

On this great open plain where the cold storm-wind plays,
Where throughout the long nights the hoarse
                                              weather-vane rasps,
Far better than in the renewed warmth of spring,
My soul will spread amply its raven-black wings.

There is nothing more sweet to the heart full of woe
And long since encrusted with hoar-frost and rime,
O dull, dreary seasons, you queens of our clime,

Than the unchanging face of your colorless gloom—
Lest it be, on a dark moonless night, two by two,
To lull dolor to sleep on a casual bed.

Le Crépuscule du matin

La diane chantait dans les cours des casernes,
Et le vent du matin soufflait sur les lanternes.

C'était l'heure où l'essaim des rêves malfaisants
Tord sur leurs oreillers les bruns adolescents;
Où, comme un œil sanglant qui palpite et qui bouge,
La lampe sur le jour fait une tache rouge;
Où l'âme, sous le poids du corps revêche et lourd,
Imite les combats de la lampe et du jour.
Comme un visage en pleurs que les brises essuient,
L'air est plein du frisson des choses qui s'enfuient,
Et l'homme est las d'écrire et la femme d'aimer.

Les maisons çà et là commençaient à fumer.
Les femmes de plaisir, la paupière livide,
Bouche ouverte, dormaient de leur sommeil stupide;
Les pauvresses, traînant leurs seins maigres et froids,
Soufflaient sur leurs tisons et soufflaient sur leurs doigts.
C'était l'heure où parmi le froid et la lésine
S'aggravent les douleurs des femmes en gésine;
Comme un sanglot coupé par un sang écumeux
Le chant du coq au loin déchirait l'air brumeux;
Une mer de brouillards baignait les édifices,
Et les agonisants dans le fond des hospices
Poussaient leur dernier râle en hoquets inégaux.
Les débauchés rentraient, brisés par leurs travaux.

L'aurore grelottante en robe rose et verte
S'avançaient lentement sur la Seine déserte,
Et le sombre Paris, en se frottant les yeux,
Empoignait ses outils, vieillard laborieux.

Daybreak

The reveille sounded in barracks courtyards,
And the street-lamps flickered in the morning wind.

'Twas the hour when, plagued by troubling dreams,
Sun-browned adolescents writhe on their beds;
When the lamp, like a bloodshot and throbbing eye,
Makes a sickly red spot on the wan light of day;
When the soul, weighted down by the gross, fretful flesh,
Seems to struggle in vain, as the lamp with the day;
Like a face wet with tears being dried by the breeze,
The air brings a shudder, a keen sense of loss,
And man wearies of writing and woman of love.

Here and there, house-chimneys were starting to smoke.
Women of pleasure, livid-lidded, lay sprawled
With their mouths gaping open, in stupefied sleep;
Beggar-women, their scrawny, cold breasts a-droop,
Were blowing on embers and blowing on hands.
'Twas the hour when women in labor, amid
Deprivation and cold, feel more keenly their pains;
Like a sob interrupted by up-foaming blood,
A distant cock's crow ripped the mist-laden air;
The buildings all swam in an ocean of fog,
And the dying sequestered in old people's homes
Were breathing their last in irregular gasps.
Debauchees, worn out by their labors, crept home.

The shivering dawn, in pale pink and green dress,
Was slowly descending the deserted Seine,
And somber grey Paris, hard-working old man,
Was rubbing his eyes, laying hold of his tools.

from the cycle
"Le Vin"

Le Vin du solitaire

Le regard singulier d'une femme galante
Qui se glisse vers nous comme le rayon blanc
Que la lune onduleuse envoie au lac tremblant
Quand elle y veut baigner sa beauté nonchalante;

Le dernier sac d'écus dans les doigts d'un joueur;
Un baiser libertin de la maigre Adeline;
Les sons d'une musique énervante et câline,
Semblable au cri lointain de l'humaine douleur,

Tout cela ne vaut pas, ô bouteille profonde,
Les baumes pénétrants que ta panse féconde
Garde au cœur altéré du poëte pieux;

Tu lui verses l'espoir, la jeunesse et la vie,
—Et l'orgueil, ce trésor de toute gueuserie,
Qui nous rend triomphants et semblables aux Dieux!

Wine of the Lonely

A streetwalker's singular, meaningful glance
Which comes wriggling toward us as does the white beam
That the undulant moon sends the trembling lake
When she chooses to bathe her cool beauty therein;

The last sack of crowns in a gambler's hand;
A hot, wanton kiss from the slim Adeline;
The cajoling of music, enervating and keen,
Like the age-old lament of humanity's pain—

All of this cannot match, O bottle profound,
The deep-healing balms that your bountiful bulge
Holds in store for the poet's devout, thirsty heart;

For him you pour hopefulness, youthfulness, life,
—And pride, that treasure in all wretchedness,
Which makes us triumphant and like unto Gods!

from the cycle
"Fleurs du mal"

Les Deux Bonnes Sœurs

La Débauche et la Mort sont deux aimables filles,
Prodigues de baisers et riches de santé,
Dont le flanc toujours vierge et drapé de guenilles
Sous l'éternel labeur n'a jamais enfanté.

Au poète sinistre, ennemi des familles,
Favori de l'enfer, courtisan mal renté,
Tombeaux et lupanars montrent sous leurs charmilles
Un lit que le remords n'a jamais fréquenté.

Et la bière et l'alcôve en blasphèmes fécondes
Nous offrent tour à tour, comme deux bonnes sœurs,
De terribles plaisirs et d'affreuses douceurs.

Quand veux-tu m'enterrer, Débauche aux bras immondes?
O Mort, quand viendras-tu, sa rivale en attraits,
Sur ses myrtes infects enter tes noirs cyprès?

The Two Kind Sisters

Two amiable wenches are Debauchery and Death,
Prodigal with kisses and robust in health,
Whose flanks, ever virgin and draped in black rags,
Under labor eternal have never begot.

To the sinister poet, the family's foe,
The minion of Hell, the hard-up sycophant,
Bawdy-houses and tombs in their snug bowers show
A bed never haunted by pangs of remorse.

Both the bier and the alcove in blasphemies rich
To us offer in turn, like two sisters benign,
Calamitous pleasures and hideous ease.

O Debauch, when will thy filthy arms bury me?
O Death, when wilt thou, her great rival in charms,
Come to graft thy black cypress on her myrtles foul?

La Fontaine de sang

Il me semble parfois que mon sang coule à flots,
Ainsi qu'une fontaine aux rhythmiques sanglots.
Je l'entends bien qui coule avec un long murmure,
Mais je me tâte en vain pour trouver la blessure.

A travers la cité, comme dans un champ clos,
Il s'en va, transformant les pavés en îlots,
Désaltérant la soif de chaque créature,
Et partout colorant en rouge la nature.

J'ai demandé souvent à des vins captieux
D'endormir pour un jour la terreur qui me mine;
Le vin rend l'œil plus clair et l'oreille plus fine!

J'ai cherché dans l'amour un sommeil oublieux;
Mais l'amour n'est pour moi qu'un matelas d'aiguilles
Fait pour donner à boire à ces cruelles filles!

The Fountain of Blood

It sometimes seems to me that my blood's gushing out
As if from a rhythmically sobbing spring;
Quite clearly I hear its prolonged gurgling flow,
But in vain grope my body in search of the wound.

All over the city, as in a walled field,
It spreads, turning paving-stones into small isles,
Assuaging the thirst of each creature that lives,
And everywhere tincturing nature with red.

I have called many times upon strong, heady wines
To allay for a day the dull gnawing of fear;
The wine clears my eye and makes keener my ear!

I have sought in love an oblivious sleep;
But for me love is only a bed of nails
Designed to give drink to those cruel girls!

La Béatrice

Dans des terrains cendreux, calcinés, sans verdure,
Comme je me plaignais un jour à la nature,
Et que de ma pensée, en vaguant au hasard,
J'aiguisais lentement sur mon cœur le poignard,
Je vis en plein midi descendre sur ma tête
Un nuage funèbre et gros d'une tempête,
Qui portait un troupeau de démons vicieux,
Semblables à des nains cruels et curieux.
A me considérer froidement ils se mirent,
Et, comme des passants sur un fou qu'ils admirent,
Je les entendis rire et chuchoter entre eux,
En échangeant maint signe et maint clignement d'yeux:

—"Contemplons à loisir cette caricature
Et cette ombre d'Hamlet imitant sa posture,
Le regard indécis et les cheveux au vent.
N'est-ce pas grand'pitié de voir ce bon vivant,
Ce gueux, cet histrion en vacances, ce drôle,
Parce qu'il sait jouer artistement son rôle,
Vouloir intéresser au chant de ses douleurs
Les aigles, les grillons, les ruisseaux et les fleurs,
Et même à nous, auteurs de ces vieilles rubriques,
Réciter en hurlant ses tirades publiques?"

J'aurais pu (mon orgueil aussi haut que les monts
Domine la nuée et le cri des démons)
Détourner simplement ma tête souveraine,
Si je ne n'eusse pas vu parmi leur troupe obscène,
Crime qui n'a pas fait chanceler le soleil!
La reine de mon cœur au regard nonpareil,
Qui riait avec eux de ma sombre détresse
Et leur versait parfois quelque sale caresse.

The Beatrice

In a cindery wasteland, barren and sear,
As I was lamenting to Nature one day,
And as slowly, while wandering at random, I honed
The dagger of thought on that whetstone, my heart,
In broad daylight I saw coming down on my head
A great murky thundercloud, bearing along
A pack of foul demons, vicious of mien,
Like malevolent, cruel, inquisitive gnomes.
Coldly they started to give me the eye,
And like bystanders jeering a madman, I heard
How they snickered and whispered amongst themselves,
While exchanging sly nudges and many a wink.

"Let's have a good look at this caricature
And shadow of Hamlet, imitating his pose,
With irresolute gaze and wild, wind-tousled hair.
What a pity to see how this playboy, this scamp,
This impostor, this out-of-work actor, this rogue,
Just because he can act out his role with such flair
Tries to interest in hearing the tale of his woes
The eagles, the crickets, the flowers and the brooks,
And harangues even us, who devised these old tricks,
With his open-air ranting, his public tirades!"

I could have just turned my head proudly aside
(My pride, soaring high as the mountains, can rise
To dominate clouds and the howling of fiends),
If among that obscene crew I hadn't espied—
O crime! Yet the sun did not stagger nor reel!—
The queen of my heart with the nonpareil eyes,
Who was laughing with them at my somber distress
And favoring each with some sordid caress.

Le Reniement de St. Pierre

Qu'est-ce que Dieu fait de ce flot d'anathèmes
Qui monte tous les jours vers ses chers séraphins?
Comme un tyran gorgé de viandes et de vins,
Il s'endort au doux bruit de nos affreux blasphèmes.

Les sanglots des martyrs et des suppliciés
Sont une symphonie enivrante sans doute,
Puisque, malgré le sang que leur volupté coûte,
Les cieux ne s'en sont point encor rassasiés.

—Ah! Jésus! souviens-toi du jardin des Olives!
Dans ta simplicité tu priais à genoux
Celui qui dans son ciel riait au bruit de clous
Que d'ignobles bourreaux plantaient dans tes chairs vives.

Lorsque tu vis cracher sur ta divinité
La crapule du corps de garde et des cuisines,
Et lorsque tu sentis s'enfoncer les épines
Dans ton crâne où vivait l'immense Humanité;

Quand de ton corps brisé la pesanteur horrible
Allongeait tes deux bras distendus, que le sang
Et la sueur coulaient de ton front pâlissant,
Quand tu fus devant tous posé comme une cible,

Rêvais-tu de ces jours si brillants et si beaux
Où tu vins pour remplir l'éternelle promesse,
Où tu foulais, monté sur une douce ânesse,
Des chemins tout jonchés de fleurs et de rameaux,

St. Peter's Denial

What does God do with the curses that rise
In a flood every day toward his dear seraphim?
Like a tyrant besotted with viands and wines,
He nods, lullabied by our blasphemous cries.

The sobs of the martyred, the screams from the rack
An enravishing symphony surely must be,
Since despite the blood shed for their pleasure thus far
The insatiable heavens still clamor for more.

Ah, Jesus! Remember Gethsemane's glade!
In your trusting simplicity, kneeling you prayed
To the One in his heaven who laughed at the sound
As base killers drove nails into your living flesh.

When you saw your divinity spat upon
By the riff-raff, the scum of the guard-house and streets;
When you felt the sharp thorns plunging into your head,
Wherein life for all vast Humanity lay;

When the terrible weight of your broken frame
Was stretching your overstrained arms, while blood
And sweat trickled down from your blanching brow;
When you hung there, a target of scorn for them all,

Did you dream of those beautiful, brilliant days
When you came the eternal promise to keep;
When astride a gentle she-donkey you trod
On ways all bestrewn with flowers and fronds;

Où, le cœur tout gonflé d'espoir et de vaillance,
Tu fouettais tous ces vils marchands à tour de bras,
Où tu fus maître enfin? Le remords n'a-t-il pas
Pénétré dans ton flanc plus avant que la lance?

Certes, je sortirai, quant à moi, satisfait
D'un monde où l'action n'est pas la sœur du rêve;
Puissé-je user du glaive et périr par le glaive.
Saint-Pierre a renié Jésus . . . il a bien fait!

When with heart swelled to bursting with courage and hope
You lashed those vile merchants with all your strength
And at last won the day? Did not, then, regret
Pierce your side even deeper than did the rude spear?

As for me, I shall be quite content to depart
From a world where the deed is not kin to the dream;
Let me live by the sword and die by the sword.
St. Peter denied Jesus—and he did right!

La Mort des pauvres

C'est la Mort qui console, hélas! et qui fait vivre;
C'est le but de la vie, et c'est le seul espoir
Qui, comme un élixir, nous monte et nous enivre,
Et nous donne le cœur de marcher jusqu'au soir;

A travers la tempête, et la neige, et le givre,
C'est la clarté vibrante à notre horizon noir;
C'est l'auberge fameuse inscrite sur le livre,
Où l'on pourra manger, et dormir, et s'asseoir;

C'est un Ange qui tient dans ses doigts magnétiques
Le sommeil et le don des rêves extatiques,
Et qui refait le lit des gens pauvres et nus;

C'est la gloire des Dieux, c'est le grenier mystique,
C'est la bourse du pauvre et sa patrie antique,
C'est le portique ouvert sur les Cieux inconnus!

Death of the Poor

It is Death which consoles us, alas, and sustains!
It's the goal of life, and the one great hope
That like an elixir, befuddles and cheers,
And gives us the heart to plod on until eve;

Through storm, snow and frost, it's the twinkling light
On our pitch-black horizon gleaming afar;
It's the famous old inn inscribed in the book,
Where one day we shall eat, and shall slumber and rest;

It's an Angel who holds in his magnetic hands
Precious sleep and the blessing of rapturous dreams,
And who remakes the bed of the naked and poor.

It's the glory of Gods, it's the mystical store,
It's the poor man's purse and his ancient home;
It's the portal of Paradise opening wide!

La Mort des artistes

Combien faut-il de fois secouer mes grelots
Et baiser ton front bas, morne caricature?
Pour piquer dans le but, de mystique nature,
Combien, ô mon carquois, perdre de javelots?

Nous userons notre âme en de subtils complots,
Et nous démolirons mainte lourde armature,
Avant de contempler la grande Créature
Dont l'infernal désir nous remplit de sanglots!

Il en est qui jamais n'ont connu leur Idole,
Et ces sculpteurs damnés et marqués d'un affront,
Qui vont se martelant la poitrine et le front,

N'ont qu'un espoir, étrange et sombre Capitole!
C'est que la Mort, planant comme un soleil nouveau,
Fera s'épanouir les fleurs de leur cerveau!

Death of Artists

How many times must I shake my bells
And kiss thy low brow, dismal caricature?
How many shafts, O my quiver, be lost
Ere I hit the impalpable, mystical mark?

We shall wear out our soul in cunning designs
And demolish many an awkward frame
Before we behold the great Creature for whom
The infernal desire fills our bosom with sobs!

There are some who never their Idol have known,
And these sculptors, condemned and branded with shame,
Who keep beating and hammering breast and brow,

Have only one hope, one strange, dark Capitol!
'Tis that Death, like a new sun afloat in the sky,
Will cause the flowers of their brain to bloom!

Le Rêve d'un curieux

Connais-tu, comme moi, la douleur savoureuse,
Et de toi fais-tu dire: "Oh! l'homme singulier!"
—J'allais mourir. C'était dans mon âme amoureuse,
Désir mêlé d'horreur, un mal particulier;

Angoisse et vif espoir, sans humeur factieuse.
Plus allait se vidant le fatal sablier,
Plus ma torture était âpre et délicieuse;
Tout mon cœur s'arrachait au monde familier.

J'étais comme l'enfant avide du spectacle,
Haïssant le rideau comme on hait un obstacle . . .
Enfin la vérité froide se révéla:

J'étais mort sans surprise, et la terrible aurore
M'enveloppait. —Eh quoi! n'est-ce donc que cela?
La toile était levée et j'attendais encore.

A Queer Fellow's Dream

Have you known, as have I, voluptuous pain,
And of you do they say: "Oh, what a queer man!"?
—I was dying. My soul brimmed with eager desire
Intermingled with horror, a trouble most strange;

Agony and bright hope, without anger or spite.
The more nearly empty the fatal hour-glass,
The keener my torture and rapture became;
My heart was torn whole from the world that I knew.

Like the child who can't wait for the show to begin,
I was hating the curtain for blocking the way . . .
At last the cold truth became clearly revealed:

I had died unawares, and the terrible dawn
Had enveloped me. —What! Is this, then, all it is?
The curtain was up, and I waited still.

Le Voyage

I

Pour l'enfant, amoureux de cartes et d'estampes,
L'univers est égal à son vaste appétit.
Ah! que le monde est grand à la clarté des lampes!
Aux yeux du souvenir que le monde est petit!

Un matin nous partons, le cerveau plein de flamme,
Le cœur gros de rancune et de désirs amers,
Et nous allons, suivant le rhythme de la lame,
Berçant notre infini sur le fini des mers.

Les uns, joyeux de fuir une patrie infâme;
D'autres, l'horreur de leurs berceaux, et quelques-uns,
Astrologues noyés dans les yeux d'une femme,
La Circé tyrannique aux dangereux parfums.

Pour n'être pas changés en bêtes, ils s'enivrent
D'espace et de lumière et de cieux embrasés;
La glace qui les mord, les soleils qui les cuivrent,
Effacent lentement la marque des baisers.

Mais les vrais voyageurs sont ceux-là qui partent
Pour partir; cœurs légers, semblables aux ballons,
De leur fatalité jamais ils ne s'écartent,
Et, sans savoir pourquoi, disent toujours: Allons!

Ceux-là dont les désirs ont la forme des nues,
Et qui rêvent, ainsi qu'un conscrit le canon,
De vastes voluptés, changeantes, inconnues,
Et dont l'esprit humain n'a jamais su le nom!

Travel

I

For the child, fascinated by pictures and maps,
The universe matches his vast appetite.
Ah, how big the world is by the light of the lamps!
By the hindsight of memory, how very small!

We sail off one morning, with brain full of fire,
Heart heavy with rancor and bitter desire,
And we rock, to the rhythmical beat of the waves,
Our infinite soul on the seas' finite breast.

Some are glad to be leaving an odious land,
Some the harsh scene of childhood—and others, a few,
Who are star-gazers drowned in the eyes of a maid,
The tyrannic Circé with her parlous perfumes.

Not to be changed to beasts, these get drunk—not on wine,
But on luminous distance and tropical skies;
The sea-wind's icy bite and the coppering sun
Will efface by degrees the deep brand of the kiss.

But the only true travelers are those who depart
For the sake of departing; hearts light as balloons,
When they're destined to travel they never demur,
But without knowing why, always say: "Let's away!"

They're the ones whose desires have shapes like the clouds
And who dream, as the new conscript dreams of the gun,
Of tremendous delights, ever-changing and strange,
And of which human minds know not even the name!

II

Nous imitons, horreur! la toupie et la boule
Dans leur valse et leurs bonds; même dans nos sommeils
La Curiosité nous tourmente et nous roule,
Comme un Ange cruel qui fouette des soleils.

Singulière fortune où le but se déplace,
Et, n'étant nulle part, peut être n'importe où!
Où l'Homme, dont jamais l'espérance n'est lasse,
Pour trouver le repos court toujours comme un fou!

Notre âme est un trois-mâts cherchant son Icarie;
Une voix retentit sur le pont: "Ouvre l'œil!"
Une voix de la hune, ardente et folle, crie:
"Amour . . . gloire . . . bonheur!" Enfer! c'est un écueil!

Chaque îlot signalé par l'homme de vigie
Est un Eldorado promis par le Destin;
L'Imagination qui dresse son orgie
Ne trouve qu'un récif aux clartés du matin.

O le pauvre amoureux des pays chimériques!
Faut-il le mettre aux fers, le jeter à la mer,
Ce matelot ivrogne, inventeur d'Amériques
Dont le mirage rend le gouffre plus amer?

Tel le vieux vagabond, piétinant dans la boue,
Rêve, le nez en l'air, de brillants paradis;
Son œil ensorcelé découvre une Capoue
Partout où la chandelle illumine un taudis.

II

We behave—horrid thought!—like the top and the ball,
Gyrating and bouncing; even when we're asleep,
Curiosity plagues us and rolls us about,
Like a merciless Angel chastising some suns.

What a strange way to live, when mercurial goals
Are established nowhere, and may be anywhere!
A life in which Man, in whom hope never flags,
Keeps on running like mad—in a search for repose!

Our soul's a three-master, Ikaria-bound;
A voice on the quarterdeck cries: "Look alive!"
A voice from the crow's-nest, impassioned and mad,
Shouts: "Love . . . glory . . . happiness!" Hell! It's a shoal!

Every island the lookout descries and reports
Is an Eldorado that's been promised by Fate;
The Fancy, constructing its orgy to come,
In the clear light of morning finds only a reef.

O the wretched admirer of fanciful lands!
Should we put him in irons, cast him into the sea,
This drunken seafarer, inventing New Worlds,
Whose mirage makes more bitter the briniest deep?

So the old vagabond, as he tramps through the mire,
With his head in the clouds, dreams of bright paradise;
His eye, being spellbound, sees Capua there
Wherever his candle illumines a shack.

III

Etonnants voyageurs! quelles nobles histoires
Nous lisons dans vos yeux profonds comme les mers!
Montrez-nous les écrins de vos riches mémoires,
Ces bijoux merveilleux, faits d'astres et d'éthers.

Nous voulons voyager sans vapeur et sans voile!
Faites, pour égayer l'ennui de nos prisons,
Passer sur nos esprits, tendus comme une toile,
Vos souvenirs avec leurs cadres d'horizons.

Dites, qu'avez-vous vu?

IV

       "Nous avons vu des astres
Et des flots; nous avons vu des sables aussi;
Et, malgré bien des chocs et d'imprévus désastres,
Nous nous sommes souvent ennuyés, comme ici.

La gloire du soleil sur la mer violette,
La gloire des cités dans le soleil couchant,
Allumaient dans nos cœurs une ardeur inquiète
De plonger dans un ciel au reflet alléchant.

Les plus riches cités, les plus grands paysages,
Jamais ne contenaient l'attrait mystérieux
De ceux que le hasard fait avec les nuages.
Et toujours le désir nous rendait soucieux!

—La jouissance ajoute au désir de la force.
Désir, vieil arbre à qui le plaisir sert d'engrais,
Cependant que grossit et durcit ton écorce,
Tes branches veulent voir le soleil de plus près!

III

Astonishing travelers! What grand, noble tales
We can read in your eyes, which are deep as the seas!
So show us the treasures your memories hold—
Those marvelous gems, wrought of ethers and stars.

We also would travel—without steam or sail!
To enliven our prison's dull boredom, transfer
To our minds, tightly stretched like a canvas, the scenes
You remember, complete with horizons for frames.

Tell us, what did you see?

IV

       "We saw planets and stars;
We saw billows and breakers, and beaches of sand;
And despite many shocks and calamities dire,
We often felt bored, as we used to do here.

The splendor of sunlight on violet seas,
The splendor of cities at sunset aglow,
Would arouse in our hearts a great yearning to plunge
Into some lovely sky whose reflection allured.

The richest of cities, the greatest landscapes
Would for us never hold the mysterious charm
Of the ones that pure chance makes appear in the clouds.
And we still felt the keen, anxious pangs of desire!

—Enjoyment just adds greater strength to desire.
O Desire, thou old tree pleasure serves to manure,
While thy bark, as time passes, becomes thick and tough,
Thy branches reach high, for close view of the sun!

Grandiras-tu toujours, grand arbre plus vivace
Que le cyprès? —Pourtant nous avons, avec soin,
Cueilli quelques croquis pour votre album vorace,
Frères qui trouvez beau tout ce qui vient de loin!

Nous avons salué des idoles à trompe;
Des trônes constellés de joyaux lumineux;
Des palais ouvragés dont la féerique pompe
Serait pour vos banquiers un rêve ruineux;

Des costumes qui sont pour les yeux une ivresse;
Des femmes dont les dents et les ongles sont teints,
Et des jongleurs savants que le serpent caresse."

V

Et puis, et puis encore?

VI

"O cerveaux enfantins!

Pour ne pas oublier la chose capitale,
Nous avons vu partout, et sans l'avoir cherché,
Du haut jusques en bas de l'échelle fatale,
Le spectacle ennuyeux de l'immortel péché:

La femme, esclave vile, orgueilleuse et stupide,
Sans rire s'adorant et s'aimant sans dégoût;
L'homme, tyran goulu, paillard, dur et cupide,
Esclave de l'esclave et ruisseau dans l'égout;

Wilt thou never stop growing, great tree more long-lived
Than the cypress? —We did, though, collect with great care
A few sketches your voracious album to fill,
You admirers of everything come from afar!

We kowtowed to idols with trunks; we beheld
Rich thrones constellated with luminous gems;
Elaborate palaces, fairy-tale pomp
That would be for your bankers a ruinous dream;

Costumes a ravishing feast for the eyes;
Women who've tinted their teeth and their nails,
And masterful jugglers by serpents caressed."

V

And what then? And what else?

VI

						"O childish brains!

Yes, we must not forget the one capital thing;
We saw everywhere, and without having sought,
From the top to the bottom of destiny's scale,
The dull, boring pageant of immortal sin;

Woman a vile slave, empty-headed and vain,
Sans humor or nausea adoring herself;
Man a gluttonous tyrant, harsh, greedy and lewd,
The slave's slave and foul path to the gutter or worse;

Le bourreau qui jouit, le martyr qui sanglote;
La fête qu'assaisonne et parfume le sang;
Le poison du pouvoir énervant le despote,
Et le peuple amoureux du fouet abrutissant;

Plusieurs religions semblables à la nôtre,
Toutes escaladant le ciel; la Sainteté,
Comme en un lit de plume un délicat se vautre,
Dans les clous et le crin cherchant la volupté;

L'Humanité bavarde, ivre de son génie,
Et folle, maintenant comme elle était jadis,
Criant à Dieu, dans sa furibonde agonie:
"O mon semblable, ô mon maître, je te maudis!"

Et les moins sots, hardis amants de la Démence,
Fuyant le grand troupeau parqué par le Destin,
Et se réfugiant dans l'opium immense!
—Tel est du globe entier l'éternel bulletin."

VII

Amer savoir, celui qu'on tire du voyage!
Le monde, monotone et petit, aujourd'hui,
Hier, demain, toujours, nous fait voir notre image:
Une oasis d'horreur dans un désert d'ennui!

Faut-il partir? rester? Si tu peux rester, reste;
Pars, s'il le faut. L'un court, et l'autre se tapit
Pour tromper l'ennemi vigilant et funeste,
Le Temps! Il est, hélas! des coureurs sans répit,

Comme le Juif errant et comme les apôtres,
A qui rien ne suffit, ni wagon ni vaisseau,

The hangman's enjoyment, the martyr's great sobs,
The festival seasoned and scented with blood;
The poison of power sapping despots of strength,
And the people grown fond of the whip's cruel lash;

Half a dozen religions resembling our own,
All ascendant to Heaven; the Holy Elite,
Like a fop wallowing in a soft feather-bed,
Seeking pleasure in badges of rank and brocade;

Mankind garrulous, glib, with its genius drunk,
And mad, as mad now as it always has been,
In its furious agony crying to God:
'O my double, my master, I call thee accursed!'

And the least stupid, daring Dementia to court,
Escaping the great herd impounded by Fate,
And taking their refuge in opium's cloud!
—That's the word for all time, from all over the globe."

VII

Bitter knowledge, that which one from travel derives!
The world, small and tiresome, today, yesterday,
Tomorrow, always, just reflects what we are:
An oasis of filth in a desert ennui!

Should one go, or remain? Stay at home if you can;
Depart if you must. Some will run, others hide,
To outwit the dread foe, ever-vigilant Time!
There are some, alas, runners who never can rest,

Like the Wandering Jew and apostles, for whom
Naught suffices, no vessel, no train, to escape

Pour fuir ce rétiaire infâme; il en est d'autres
Qui savent le tuer sans quitter leur berceau.

Lorsque enfin il mettra le pied sur notre échine,
Nous pourrons espérer et crier: En avant!
De même qu'autrefois nous partions pour la Chine,
Les yeux fixés au large et les cheveux au vent.

Nous nous embarquerons sur la mer des Ténèbres
Avec le cœur joyeux d'un jeune passager.
Entendez-vous ces voix, charmantes et funèbres,
Qui chantent: "Par ici! vous qui voulez manger

Le Lotus parfumé! c'est ici qu'on vendange
Les fruits miraculeux dont votre cœur a faim;
Venez vous enivrer de la douceur étrange
De cette après-midi qui n'a jamais de fin!"

A l'accent familier nous devinons le spectre;
Nos Pylades là-bas tendent leurs bras vers nous.
"Pour rafraîchir ton cœur nage vers ton Electre!"
Dit celle dont jadis nous baisions les genoux.

VIII

O Mort, vieux capitaine, il est temps! levons l'ancre!
Ce pays nous ennuie, ô Mort! Appareillons!
Si le ciel et la mer sont noirs comme de l'encre,
Nos cœurs que tu connais sont remplis de rayons!

Verse-nous ton poison pour qu'il nous réconforte!
Nous voulons, tant ce feu nous brûle le cerveau,
Plonger au fond du gouffre, Enfer ou Ciel, qu'importe?
Au fond de l'Inconnu pour trouver du *nouveau*!

From that infamous web-thrower; others there are
Who can kill him without ever leaving their crib.

When he finally does plant his foot on our spine,
We can hope and cry: "Forward! Onward! Away!"
Just as in the old days we would sail for Cathay
With our eyes fixed to seaward and hair to the wind.

On the Ocean of Darkness we'll gaily embark
With the gladness of heart of a passenger youth.
Do you hear them, those voices, enticing, deep-toned,
That keep chanting: "This way, you who long to partake

Of the sweet-scented Lotus! It's gathered right here,
That miraculous fruit that your heart hungers for;
Come and put yourself under the strange, drunken spell
Of this long afternoon stretching on without end!"?

The accent's familiar—we divine who it is;
Our Pylades over there hold their arms out to us.
"Swim toward your Electra, refreshen your heart!"
Says that woman whose knees long ago we would kiss.

VIII

O Death, old sea-captain, it's time! Let's weigh anchor!
We fret at this sojourn, O Death! Let's set sail!
Though the sky and the sea be as dark as black ink,
Our hearts, as you know, are aglow with bright rays!

So pour us your lethal, all-comforting draft!
Our brains are on fire; we are eager to plunge
Deep into the abyss—Hell or Heaven, what odds?
Deep into the Unknown, just to find something *new*!

*Selected
miscellaneous
poems*

Le Coucher du soleil romantique

Que le soleil est beau quand tout frais il se lève,
Comme une explosion nous lançant son bonjour!
—Bienheureux celui-là qui peut avec amour
Saluer son coucher plus glorieux qu'un rêve!

Je me souviens! . . . J'ai vu tout, fleur, source, sillon,
Se pâmer sous son œil comme un cœur qui palpite . . .
—Courons vers l'horizon, il est tard, courons vite,
Pour attraper au moins un oblique rayon!

Mais je poursuis en vain le Dieu qui se retire;
L'irrésistible Nuit établit son empire,
Noire, humide, funeste et pleine de frissons;

Une odeur de tombeau dans les ténèbres nage,
Et mon pied peureux froisse, au bord du marécage,
Des crapauds imprévus et de froids limaçons.

Romantic Sunset

How fine is the sun when he rises afresh
Like a great burst of fireworks to bid us good day!
—Thrice blest whosoever can lovingly hail
His setting, resplendent beyond any dream!

I remember! . . . how furrow, flower and rill
All basked in his glance like a beating heart . . .
—Let's run westward, and quickly, before it's too late,
To catch at least one of his last oblique rays!

But in vain I pursue the withdrawing God;
Irresistible Night has established her sway,
Dark, humid and baneful, all shudders and dread;

In the darkness there floats a whiff of the grave,
And my fearful foot treads, at the brink of the fen,
On startling toads and on cold, clammy snails.

A une Malabaraise

Tes pieds sont aussi fins que tes mains et ta hanche
Est large à faire envie à la plus belle blanche;
A l'artiste pensif ton corps est doux et cher;
Tes grands yeux de velours sont plus noirs que ta chair.
Aux pays chauds et bleus où ton Dieu t'a fait naître,
Ta tâche est d'allumer la pipe de ton maître,
De pourvoir les flacons d'eau fraîches et d'odeurs,
De chasser loin du lit les moustiques rôdeurs,
Et, dès que le matin fait chanter les platanes,
D'acheter au bazar ananas et bananes.
Tout le jour, où tu veux, tu mènes tes pieds nus,
Et fredonnes tout bas de vieux airs inconnus;
Et quand descend le soir au manteau d'écarlate,
Tu poses doucement ton corps sur une natte,
Où tes rêves flottants sont pleins de colibris,
Et toujours, comme toi, gracieux et fleuris.

Pourquoi, l'heureuse enfant, veux-tu voir notre France,
Ce pays trop peuplé que fauche la souffrance,
Et, confiant ta vie aux bras forts des marins,
Faire de grands adieux à tes chers tamarins?
Toi, vêtue à moitié de mousselines frêles,
Frissonnante là-bas sous la neige et les grêles,
Comme tu pleurerais tes loisirs doux et francs,
Si, le corset brutal emprisonnant tes flancs,
Il te fallait glaner ton souper dans nos fanges
Et vendre le parfum de tes charmes étranges,
L'œil pensif, et suivant, dans nos sales brouillards,
Des cocotiers absents les fantômes épars!

To a Malabar Girl

Your small feet are as fine as your hands, and your hips
Broad enough to make envious any white belle;
Your form, to an artist, is priceless and sweet;
Your great velvet eyes darker brown than your skin.
In the warm, sunny land where your God gave you life,
Your tasks are to kindle your master's filled pipe,
To replenish the jars with fresh water and scent,
To chase roving mosquitoes away from the beds,
And when morning winds cause the plane-trees to sing,
To buy mangoes and pineapples in the bazaar.
All day long you go, barefoot, wherever you like,
Contentedly humming your curious old tunes;
And when night with its mantle of scarlet descends,
You dispose yourself quietly on a straw mat,
Where your untroubled dreams are of bright humming-birds,
And like you, always dainty and flower-bedecked.

Oh why, happy child, should you crave to see France,
That too-populous country where suffering's rife,
And, entrusting your life to the sailors' strong arms,
Bid reluctant farewell to your dear marmosets?
Semi-clad as you are in a thin muslin dress,
Shivering over there in the snow and the hail,
How you'd weep for your free, pleasant, leisurely life
If, with brutal tight corsets confining your flanks,
You were forced to subsist on our refuse and vice,
And to sell the exotic bouquet of your charms,
Nostalgically seeking, in our wretched fogs,
The sparse apparitions of faraway palms!

N'est-ce pas qu'il est doux, maintenant que nous sommes
Fatigués et flétris comme les autres hommes,
De chercher quelquefois à l'Orient lointain
Si nous voyons encor les rougeurs du matin,
Et, quand nous avançons dans la rude carrière,
D'écouter les échos qui chantent en arrière
Et les chuchotements de ces jeunes amours
Que le Seigneur a mis au début de nos jours?

Retrospect

Is it not sweet for us, now that we have become
Fatigued and wilted by the years like other men,
To look back now and then toward the distant East
For what we still can see of morning's rosy glow,
And, when we're far advanced along the rugged path,
To hearken to the echoes drifting back to us,
And to the whispers of those passionate young loves
The Lord vouchsafed to grant us early in our days?

Hymne

A la très-chère, à la très-belle
Qui remplit mon cœur de clarté,
A l'ange, à l'idole immortelle,
Salut en immortalité!

Elle se répand dans ma vie
Comme un air imprégné de sel,
Et dans mon âme inassouvie
Verse le goût de l'éternel.

Sachet toujours frais qui parfume
L'atmosphère d'un cher réduit,
Encensoir oublié qui fume
En secret à travers la nuit,

Comment, amour incorruptible,
T'exprimer avec vérité?
Grain de musc qui gis, invisible,
Au fond de mon éternité!

A la très-bonne, à la très-belle
Qui fait ma joie et ma santé,
A l'ange, à l'idole immortelle,
Salut en immortalité!

Hymn

To her most dear, to her most fair
Who fills my heart with radiant light,
Immortal idol, angel bright,
All hail, to immortality!

She permeates through all my life
Like air impregnated with salt,
And into my unsated soul
The taste of the eternal pours.

Still-fresh sachet that keeps perfumed
The air of a beloved retreat,
Forgotten censer left to smoke
In secret on throughout the night,

Love incorruptible—how to
Express most truly what you are?
A grain of musk, you lie unseen
Deep down in my eternal core!

To her most sweet, to her most fair
Who makes my happiness and health,
Immortal idol, angel bright,
All hail, to immortality!

NOTES ON THE TRANSLATIONS

"To the Reader": As the opening gambit of *Les Fleurs du mal*, this provocative manifesto sets the tone for what has been called Baudelaire's "poetry of sin." . . . In stanza 3, some possible alternatives: "bewitched" for "enthralled," and "erudite" for "masterful." For the sake of metric regularity and euphony, "nous nous faisons payer grassement nos aveux" has been rendered somewhat freely, and "le riche métal" expanded descriptively. . . For "canevas," "counterpane" is a loose rendition made primarily for meter; but its association with sleep is also suggestive of the lack of excitement in "nos piteux destins." . . . "Hyenas" not only fits the meter better than would "jackals," but also—deservedly or not— connotes more vividly for most people the morally and physically repulsive scavenger. . . . In stanza 8, the four successive participial modifiers present a special problem. With three of them converted into verbs, "grognants" is obliquely rendered by "slavering," a word whose overtones seem particularly effective in this context.

"Benediction": From the tenor of the first five stanzas, one may safely assume that this poem was not among the favorites of Baudelaire's mother. . . . In stanza 6, "like that of the gods" is a semantic overkill, made necessary by the meter. Although the word "vermeil" is thereby lost, "nectar" in English is better off without the adjective. . . . Verbal phrases such as "s'enivre" in stanzas 6 and 7 and "me soûlerai" in stanza 11 almost always have to be paraphrased, because "to get drunk" and all its English equivalents are either awkwardly polysyllabic (e.g., "intoxicated") or else too pejorative for figurative context. In this connection, see also the note below on "l'homme ivre" in the poem "Les Hiboux." . . . Stanza 14 poses the recurrent problem of how to render "esprit": should it be "mind" or "spirit"? Although the latter has been chosen in this instance, on the assumption that the poet's "esprit lucide" transcends intellect, "luminous mind" would nevertheless be an acceptable alternative to "spirit's clear flame." . . . . Students of angelology will recognize the Virtues, Dominions and Thrones as categories of angels in the heavenly hierarchy.

"The Albatross": Although the poet does not immediately concentrate his attention on a single albatross, the stylistic and metrical problems posed by his plurals in the first two stanzas make it expedient to use the singular throughout, with only "whose kind" in line 3 as acknowledgment. . . .

"Deposed" could just as well be "set down," since "déposer" has both meanings; but "deposed" is preferred because the albatross is a "king" in the next line. . . . For "lui, naguère si beau," strict translation has proved impractical; hence the rhetorical question: "Where now is his beauty?" . . . "Marooned" in the final couplet is, undeniably, a dangling participle. The syntax could be corrected by changing the last line to "He cannot walk for his vast giant's wings"; but to do so would entail the disproportionate sacrifice of the closing rhyme. Besides, Baudelaire's "exilé" has precisely the same syntactic flaw.

"Elevation": Since "au-dessus de" has twice as many syllables as "above," the renditions of "étangs" and "vallées" have been expanded, in order to maintain the metrical balance of the opening line. . . . Normally it would be preferable to render "tu" as "thou" in a context where the poet is addressing his own spirit, as in lines 5 and 7; but in this case the archaic verb forms thereby required, "movest" and "dost furrow," would be detrimental to euphony. . . . As a modifier of "existence," the figurative adjective "brumeuse" (literally "foggy") obviously suggests an obscurity of meaning or purpose. A figurative "opaque," however, is preferred over "obscure," since in English usage an "obscure existence" is something quite different: namely, an inconspicuous or undistinguished existence. . . . "Midsummer" is a semantically innocuous addition, to remedy the disparity in syllable count between "alouettes" and "larks."

"Correspondences": In this translation, several words have been expanded for the sake of meter, most of them adjectives; "confuses," "familiers," "frais," "doux" and "verts." In the latter three instances, the respective sensual impressions involved (feel, sound and color) have served as a guiding principle in selection of appropriate adjectives to be added: "fresh and cool," "clear and dulcet," "soft green." . . . Although the meter of line 13 would be a little more regular if the order of "musk and incense" were reversed, this order is preferred because it preserves a closing rhyme.

"The Beacons": In this poem, Baudelaire's capsule characterizations of painters he considers immortal reflect his keen interest in painting and his perceptiveness as an art critic. His favorite among contemporary painters was Delacroix, whose work did not at first meet with widespread approval. . . . "Weber" in stanza 8 would be Karl Maria Friedrich Ernst von Weber, a German composer of romantic opera and instrumental music, very popular in Baudelaire's time. . . . The word "mille," occurring repeatedly in stanzas 9 and 10, poses an unusual problem: that of coping with the additonal syllables in "thousands of." Normally it is the English which is more economical of syllables.

"The Bad Monk": The self-castigating tone of this poem is characteristic of Baudelaire's chronic anxiety and frustration over his own shortcomings.

"The Foe": Some words and phrases added here for the sake of meter are "raging," "and harm," "and leached," "deadly" and "still." Whenever this technique is employed, there is admittedly some loss of Baudelaire's poetic concision; but rhythmic integrity is considered to be the higher of these two values. Such metrical "padding" should introduce no extraneous semantic element—no concept which is not at least implied by the French. It can sometimes serve to intensify or vivify the imagery, as the words "raging," "leached" and "deadly" do in this instance.

"Ill-Starred": The compound adjective "secret-sweet" derives from a visceral feeling that "doux comme un secret" is intended to be a semantic unit. If this interpretation is mistaken—that is, if "comme un secret" is merely an adverbial phrase modifying "épanche"—then this line should be rendered as "Wafts forth its fragrance secretly." . . . In the sestet, Baudelaire has clearly borrowed a concept from Thomas Gray's "Elegy Written in a Country Churchyard."

"The Previous Life": "Les soleils marins" might be more directly rendered as "the maritime suns," which would also be metrically satisfactory; but "the suns and the sea" seems more vivid and euphonious. The logical inference in this phrase is that the "mille feux" which color these "vastes portiques" result from the varied effects of sunlight reflected off the sea, at different seasons and times of day. . . . Baudelaire's concept of the fusion of different sensual impressions, most clearly enunciated in "Correspondances," recurs in lines 5-8 of this poem.

"Gypsies on the Move": The difficulty of rendering adequately the phrase "l'empire familier" has called for some reorganization of the closing lines.

"Man and the Sea": In line 4 the "esprit" dilemma once again presents itself. This time "mind" is preferred over "spirit" because it makes for a more clear-cut distinction from "soul" in line 2. . . . The most difficult problem in this translation is that presented by the two lines in stanza 3 apostrophizing the two antagonists and involving the "nul ne . . ." construction. . . . A viable alternative to "sans pity or qualm" would be "inexorably," interpreting "sans pitié ni remord" as a more closely-knit idiomatic construction.

"Beauty": Here the poet assumes the voice of a white marble statue of Venus, in an oudoor setting.

"The Giantess": This sonnet is a good example of Baudelaire's often-cited penchant for strange, outlandish concepts, expressed in impeccably poetic language. Other poems in this book which might fall into the same category include "La Cloche fêlée," "La Fontaine de sang" and "La Béatrice."

"Exotic Perfume": Another Baudelairian exercise in the blending of physical sensations.

"De profundis clamavi": This title could of course be Anglicized into something like "A Cry from the Depths"; but no purpose seems to be served by changing it from the neutral Latin. . . . "Lies entombed" is admittedly a loose rendition of "est tombé"; but it solves a rather difficult metrical problem and provides a near-rhyme with "gloom.."

"Evening Harmony": The slow music of these four quatrains, with lines 2 and 4 of each being repeated as lines 1 and 3 of the next, suggests the deliberate, contrapuntal tolling of church-bells. . . . The rhyming of the ecclesiastical terms "encensoir," "reposoir" and "ostensoir" is so essential to this music that the latter two words, which lack manageable English equivalents, have been left in the French, with explanatory footnotes following.

"The Phial": Some translators of this poem have rendered "flacon" as "flagon" or "flask," making it sound like a receptacle for certain prosaic alcoholic beverages rather than one for potent, esoteric perfumes. "Phial" is preferred over "vial" because its relative rarity gives it slightly more exotic overtones. . . . For "on dirait," a metrically equivalent alternative to "it's as if" would be the direct rendition "one would say." This might, however, be susceptible to the objection that "it sounds like a translation." . . . In the phrase "une âme qui revient," it is the verb that suggests a ghost ("un revenant").... In line 11, metrical considerations account for the expansion of "dégagent" to "unfold and deploy" and the addition of the adjective "sheer," which is compatible with the poet's "emerging butterflies" image.... For any Baudelaire translator, it is very fortunate that "gouffre," one of the poet's favorite words, has a number of English near-equivalents with differing metrical and phonic characteristics. In addition to "chasm" and "gulf," used here in lines 16 and 17 respectively, there are also "abyss" (used in the closing lines of "Travel"), "pit" (used in "The Clock"), and "deeps" (used in "The Albatross").

"Invitation to the Voyage": For the somewhat cryptic "miroirs profonds," the rendition "deep-banked / Mirrors" is intended to suggest that the effect of depth would be achieved by the arrangement of mirrors in sets or banks, in such a way that their reflections would repeat and reinforce each other.

"Autumn Song": Although "grim" is a word not normally used to describe the quality of a sound, it is preferred here over "muffled" or "hollow" not only for proper syllable count, but also because what is "sourd" here is not the sound itself, but its "echo"—that is, its implications for the hearer. These are certainly "grim." . . . In the opening line of Part II, "almond" is added primarily to clarify the imagery of "vos longs yeux." To describe a person's eyes simply as "long" in English seems awkward to the point of being unclear..... For "genoux," "lap" is preferred over "knees" as a comfortable resting-place for the poet's "front"; and the latter word is interpreted as synecdoche for "tête." These renditions make it possible to avoid the ludicrous, "face-down" visual imagery of "forehead on knees."

"To a Creole Lady": The first stanza of this poem presents many difficulties, not the least of which is a stern test of the translator's determination to retain the poet's imagery. The temptation is strong to "improve" line 3 by substituting a simplified paraphrase: "And of languorous, somnolent palms, . . ." In "charmes ignorés," the poet clearly has in mind a certain unfamiliar, exotic quality in the lady's beauty; but since neither of these adjectives scans well with "charms," the somewhat reluctant choice is "singular." . . .Most translators have rendered "brune" as "brown" or "dusky," giving the impression that this "enchanteresse" is of native or mixed blood. Paul Robert's *Dictionnaire de la langue française*, however, defines "brun" (of persons) as "having dark hair (or complexion)"; and this lady's coloring is "pâle." The same dictionary defines "créole" as "a person of the white race, born in the inter-tropical colonies." Note also that the subject apparently owns black slaves. . . .The French word "manoir," a clear-enough cognate of "manor," is retained for the sake of both rhythm and rhyme. As a non-rhyming alternative, "chateau" would be metrically satisfactory; but as an English word it would sound a bit too grand.

"Moon-Tears": In the absence of any point of comparison, "avec plus de paresse" apparently implies "more . . . than usual": hence "most." . . . Although a direct rendition of "l'azur" as "the blue" would suit the meter nicely, describing a nocturnal sky as "blue" (let alone "azure") rings less than true in English. "Night" has the additional advantage of creating a rhyme.

"Cats": This is one of several poems in which Baudelaire reveals that he had a strong affection and admiration for cats. . . . An interesting alternative to "reclining" would be the heraldic term "couchant," which is precisely descriptive of the sphinx's head-up physical attitude. Its overtones of formal stylization are not at all inappropriate here; but "couchant" is less pleasing metrically than "reclining," and is perhaps a bit *recherché* for the simple word "allongés."

"Owls": The basic denotation of "rangés" is of course "lined up," and most translators have taken it at this apparent face value. But the word is also used (especially of children) to mean "orderly" or "well-behaved." In this more likely vein, "solemn and sedate" offers the welcome bonus of alliteration and of rhyme with the subsequent "meditate." . . .Rendition of the difficult phrase "l'homme ivre de" as "whoso will . . . chase" is admittedly oblique; but the progression from "being drunk with" passing shadows to pursuing them is a quite logical one.

"Interment": In this version, the demands of clarity and euphony have led not only to some additions and expansions for the sake of meter ("drowsy grow," "poor," "dire," "foul" and "flesh-and-bone"), but also to the shifting of "inters" forward to line 2, where it creates a near-rhyme with "yours." This same shift necessitates the condensation of "un bon chrétien, par charité" into "some good Samaritan."

"The Happy Corpse": The opening word "somewhere" is by no means a gratuitous addition. It is clearly needed in order to render "une terre grasse" correctly, and it derives specifically from the indefinite article. Other examples of this phenomenon occur in "Spleen" (I), (II), and (III) respectively: "some dropsical old woman's," "some hazy Sahara" and "some pluvious land." . . . Several translators have used the word "grave" to render "fosse," whereas that word's basic denotation and the self-deprecating tone of this poem clearly demand something matter-of-fact and without emotional overtones, such as "ditch," "trench" or "pit." This probably illustrates how the demands of rhyme in the target language can exert a negative influence on the fidelity of a translation; for in these cases, a forthcoming rhyme with "wave" must have figured in the word choice of each translator. . . . "Epicurean" is preferred over "hedonistic" (its virtual synonym and metrical equivalent) because it suggests a little more effectively the gustatory aspect of these philosophers' pleasure-seeking. An intriguing alternative, in the same vein, would be "You gourmet philosophers." . . . For "mort parmi les morts," a literal rendition as "dead among the dead" would be less than clear. "More dead than alive," while oblique and intuitive, seems ideally suited to the tone and context of the poem.

"The Cracked Bell": "Sous la tente," in military parlance, means "en bivouac" or "in the field," which the word "sentinel" is intended to suggest. As an alternative, "on watch in the field" would scan satisfactorily, but might be somewhat less clear to most readers. . . . "Dans d'immenses efforts" is a phrase which defies direct translation and has given many a translator plenty of trouble. "Every muscle astrain" is commended to the reader's attention.

"Late January": The French word "Pluviôse," the name of a winter month of France's short-lived Revolutionary calendar embracing late January and early February, is retained for its special effect. Its meaning should be sufficiently clear from the "translated" title. . . . One may suppose that the "old poet's soul" which wails from the rainspout is the wintry wind.

"The Sphinx": The author's translation of this poem, being the first one he ever attempted, has quite understandably undergone more revision than any other. Not a single line remains as it was originally rendered. . . . The single-line opening "stanza," straightforward in French and relatively easy to render into English of similar length and rhythm, has suffered many indignities at the hands of translators. . . . In this oblique rendition of "sous les lourds flocons des neigeuses années," the double meaning of the verb "drift" is a welcome dividend.

. . . For a comment on the near-rhymes in lines 17-18 and 20-21, see notes below on *Tædium vitæ*.

"Tædium vitæ": Since French prosody requires that each poetic line end on a stressed syllable, dactylic English words such as "falconry" and "balcony" are normally to be avoided at the end of a line. In this instance, however, "balcony" seems virtually unavoidable in that position; so "not hunting, nor falconry" is preferred over "not the hunt, nor the hawk," since it creates a near-rhyme. . . . In "The Sphinx," a similar rationale accounts for the lines ending in "apathy" and "immortality" and in "terror" and "Sahara."

"Despair": Line 2 of stanza 2 provides a striking example of the disparity in number of syllables which may be involved in translating a phrase directly from French to English. "Où l'Espérance, comme une chauve-souris," thanks to some operative mute *e*'s, fills out an entire 12- syllable line, whereas its direct English equivalent, "Where Hope, like a bat," constitutes only five syllables. Expansion of the English to maintain the meter is of course less difficult than condensation would be. In this instance, "fluttering" and "in the gloom" have been added, effectively reinforcing the imagery of "bat" and "dungeon" without making any significant semantic addition. . . . For "se cognant," such possible renditions as "bumping" and "knocking" have been rejected in favor of "bruising," for the sake of the latter's emotional overtones. "Plafonds pourris" has required some rationalization, since stone prison ceilings are unlikely to be "rotten." . . . In stanza 3 "murky" and "thick" are logical extensions of "vast prison" and "bars," added gratuitously for the sake of meter. "Damp," likewise added primarily for meter, is consistent with this stanza's "rain" motif; and in conjunction with "webs" it provides some consonantal repetition with "spin," "depths" and "brains."

"Obsession": One aspect of Baudelaire's thoroughly non-Romantic attitude toward Nature is clearly displayed in this poem. . . . For "maudits," the oblique rendition "stricken" is preferred over the more direct "cursed," whose effect in this context would be a bit too strong. . . . In this rendition of "le rire énorme de la mer," the reader may be taken aback by the word "guffaw." This rendition has been made, however, in conscious emulation of Baudelaire's practice of introducing a rough, crude element into an otherwise impeccably crafted poetic line. Note in this connection the word "gosier" in line 14 of "L'Horloge."

"Taste for Oblivion": Baudelaire's love of music surfaces clearly in lines 8-9 of this poem. Although not a trained musician, he had an intuitive flair for analyzing and critically appraising music. He was one of the few critics to praise the work of Richard Wagner when that composer's new music was being ridiculed throughout Europe. . . . A direct rendition of "adorable" has been avoided because of the overtones of gushy insincerity which that word has acquired in English. . . . The synecdochical "wall" is preferred over "hut" for the sake of the closing rhyme.

"The Self-Tormentor": The indicated unorthodox pronunciation of "Sahara" is of course prompted by a concern for metric consistency. This can hardly be considered an abuse of poetic license, since "Sahará" merely retains the French stress. . . . For "sinistre miroir," the rendition initially considered was "evil looking-glass," which would be comfortable, both metrically and stylistically. "Sinister," however, has been deemed preferable to "evil" because of its "left-handed" derivation suggesting "misbegotten," "unlucky," etc.; this seems more appropriate for a hapless victim of Irony. . . . One alternative rendition of lines 21-22 would be: "I am the wound, and yet the knife! / I am the slap, and yet the cheek!" Another would substitute "also" for "and yet" in each of the above lines. But because of the comma stops required in these renditions, they would lack the immediacy of Baudelaire's antithetical pairings.

"The Clock": Although it is a rather loose rendition of "fuira vers l'horizon," "will fade from the scene" has the advantage of supporting the ballet-theater simile in the following line, where the verb "flee" is recovered. . . . "Plein d'effroi" in line 3 has been misread by a number of translators as "fearful" or "afraid" instead of "frightful" or "fearsome." This has led them into the further error of assuming that "dans ton cœur plein d'effroi" modifies "se planteront." The net result is that their versions give the patently erroneous impression that the clock-god will suffer the "vibrantes Douleurs" instead of inflicting them. . . . Although "water-clock," a far less recondite word, would be both semantically and metrically equivalent to "clepsydra," the latter is preferred for its flavorful similarity to the French word.

"Landscape": The initial rendition of this version ended its first line with "lines to compose," on the theory that Baudelaire's selection of the word "églogues" was probably due to his need of a rhyme with "astrologues," rather than to any view of himself as primarily a composer of pastoral idylls; but since the tone of this poem is so unwontedly cheerful, such a supposition may not be valid. At any rate, this more direct rendition requires no such rationalization.

"The Sun": In lines 7-8, "Trébuchant sur" and "Heurtant" are semantically close enough to each other to warrant this single-verb rendition: "Stumbling over . . ./ And . . . upon . . ." . . .For "hôpitaux" in the closing line, the rendition "poorhouse" is based on Robert's definition of "hôpital" (now labeled *obsolete*, but not necessarily so in Baudelaire's time) as "a charitable establishment where persons without resources are taken in, supported and cared for." "Poorhouse" is preferred over "hospital" because it pairs more logically with "chateau," suggesting "the poor and the rich" rather than "the sick and the rich."

"The Seven Old Men": For "sinistre vieillard" in stanza 9, "evil old scoundrel" is a tempting alternative rendition; but the adjective "sinister" retains the exact nuance of its French cognate, suggesting evil without declaring it overtly. . . . In stanza 11, metrical considerations have called for retaining the French word "fatal" (cf. "femme fatale") to provide a stressed line-ending syllable, and for indicating a Gallicized pronunciation of "Phœnix."

"The Blind": The word "stiff," consistent with the "mannequins" image, has been added in order to provide an accented syllable at the end of line 2. . . . Despite the clarity of the visual image it conveys, "dardant on ne sait où" is by no means an easy phrase to render, since the verb "darder" normally means "to hurl" or "to throw," as one hurls or throws a dart; but "rolling . . . this way and that" should describe adequately the seemingly random movement of sightless eyes.

"A Woman Passing By": This is one of the poems in which use of "thou" for the familiar form would have necessitated too many unfamiliar, antiquated verbs. (See notes on "Le Reniement de St. Pierre," below.) . . . "Le plaisir qui tue" obviously refers to sexual attraction.

"Nightfall": This poem and "Le Crépuscule du matin" are among the many which reflect Baudelaire's compassion for humble, disadvantaged people and his sensitive awareness of the unhappiness of their lives. . . . The gratuitous little dig at "men of affairs" may possibly indicate the poet's resentment of such people as his financial counselor and his publishers, whom he may have held partly responsible for keeping him constantly in financial difficulty. . . . For "maîtresses," the off-beat word "jills" has been selected, in part, for the rhyme it effects.

"Love of the Lie": In line 9, "je me dis" has been reduced to "I think," since the five syllables of "I say to myself" would take up so much of the line that its remaining concepts could not be accommodated. . . . In line 19, maintaining the desired meter has called for some extraordinary measures, most of which involve economy of syllables. "Beaux écrins" has been rendered simply as "jewel-cases," whose beauty remains only implied; the one-syllable "sans" has been used twice instead of "without"; and both "médaillons" and "reliques" have been rendered obliquely, and jointly, in the word "reliquaries," which contains the essential semantic core of both the French words. Meanwhile "bones" (which are among the relics most often kept in reliquaries) provides the desired line-ending stressed syllable. . . . Although a dictionary search has yielded no specific mention of "morbide attrait," there are some compelling reasons for reading this phrase as "beauty-spot" (a mole or other small blemish, either real or artificial, which by contrast heightens the beauty of a woman's complexion). (1) Stylistically, the position of the descriptive adjective "morbide" before its noun strongly suggests an idiomatic, non-literal usage. (2) This interpretation is inherently logical: an ugly mole on an otherwise beautiful complexion is indeed morbidly fascinating to the onlooker. (3) Morphologically, these two phrases closely resemble each other; their internal semantic tension is almost identical in nature and degree. That is, "morbide" clashes with "attrait" in the same way as "beauty" clashes with "spot." (4) Finally, the context is firmly supportive: by what else but such a beauty-spot could this "front pâle" possibly be "embelli"? . . . For "stupid, indifferent," an acceptable alternative would be "stupid and spiritless."

"The Nanny": For "servante," the specific term "nanny" is preferred over "servant girl" or "maidservant, " because the poet's nostalgic memories of this dead woman and his sense of obligation to her, together with his mother's onetime jealousy of her, make it plain that she had been his childhood nurse. . . . For "quelques fleurs," the rendition "flowers now and then" attributes to "quelques" something more than its basic denotation of "some" or "a few." It is logical to infer that the poet's feelings of guilt would never have been assuaged by a single visit to the cemetery, and therefore that "quelques" is intended

to have an iterative effect. . . . In line 7, the non-standard spelling of "certes" without its final -*s* clearly indicates that this particular mute -*e*, despite the comma which sets it off visually, is not to be pronounced as one of the counted twelve syllables, but is to be absorbed into the following vowel sound of "ils."

"Fogs and Rains": For "un vague tombeau," the essential rendition is "a kind of tomb." The word "gray," consistent with the visual imagery, is added to improve the meter. . . . "Pâles ténèbres" is a phrase which is certainly not susceptible to offhand, "literal" translation. "Pale darkness" would be almost unintelligible. . . . Since "la douleur" is non-specific in this context, "dolor," whose very rarity makes it sound somewhat vague, is preferred over its metrical equivalent "sorrow," which seems to imply a specific cause.

"Daybreak": The difficulty of the phrase "le frisson des choses qui s'enfuient" has called for the stratagem of breaking it up into two components. . . . For "dans le fond des" in line 22, any direct rendition such as "in the depths of" would sound at best like "translatese," while a simple preposition such as "within" or "inside" would not adequately convey the sense of isolation implicit in this phrase. Fortunately, "sequestered in" proves metrically compatible.

"Wine of the Lonely": This poem's most difficult line for the translator is "les sons d'une musique énervante et câline," juxtaposing as it does two very disparate adjectives. . . . The word "pieux," used here as in other poems to modify "le poëte," clearly implies devotion to poetry, rather than religious piety.

"The Two Kind Sisters": In this poem we have one of the best ex-amples of Baudelaire's talent for making poetic capital of his own feelings of guilt and degradation, after having yielded to human weakness. It also illustrates the near-obsession with death which was a factor in his unpopularity. . . . Lines 5-6 offer some clues to his appraisal of the prevailing public attitude toward poets like himself.

"The Fountain of Blood": Interpretation and rendition of the final word "filles" are rather difficult. Some translators have rendered it as "whores," the tone of which seems inappropriate, since the context suggests at least some degree of emotional involvement. "Women" is unsuitable on several counts, including meter. "Girls," while less than ideal because of its connotation of juvenility, at least provides consonance with "nails" in the preceding line. . . . Surprisingly, the rendition "bed of nails" for "matelas d'aiguilles" has been found in no other translator's version.

"The Beatrice": For "calcinés" in the opening line, the word "sear," somewhat rare as an adjective, is preferred over its homonym "sere" because it suggests "burnt" or "scorched" rather than "dried up" or "withered." The word in the context which determines this choice is, of course, "cendreux."

"St. Peter's Denial": The familiar pronouns and adjectives "tu," "ton," etc. always pose the problem of whether or not to render them as "thou" and "thy." In this case the decision in the negative was an easy one to make, since to do so would have entailed using a number of awkward, archaic verb forms to impede the poem's easy flow. . . . A different decision has been made in translating poems where the familiar form occurs only once or twice, and is without verbal complication, such as "*De profundis clamavi*" and "The Sphinx."

"Death of the Poor": In the opening line of this poem, the exclamation point has been arbitrarily relocated, since the occurrence of such a punctuation mark in mid-sentence tends to be more disruptive in English style than in French. . . . In line 3 it has proved possible, for once, to find a suitable (albeit unusual) rendition for the verb "enivre," without resorting to paraphrase.

"Death of Artists": Just as the court jester shakes his bells to please his royal master, the would-be artist suffers humiliation to placate his deity, Art. . . . "Sculpteurs" here is of course metaphorical, referring to toilers in all the arts, including poetry, who "keep beating . . . breast and brow" ("hammering" themselves like sculptors) because they have never achieved their artistic ideal. . . . The cryptic "Capitole" probably alludes to Rome's Capitoline Hill, associated with the "triumph" or celebration of success.

"A Queer Fellow's Dream": The "humeur factieuse" which is absent from the poet's "mal particulier" could be the resentful anger so often reported by those who have faced imminent death. . . . In earlier drafts of this version, "m'enveloppait" was rendered as "enveloped me," employing the least unsuitable of the tenses usually used to render the *imparfait*. "Had enveloped me," however, is much more satisfying.

Although past perfect, it implies very clearly the resultant descriptive condition.

"Travel": This poem reveals quite clearly that Baudelaire did not share the Romantic predilection for glamorous, exotic places. Apparently the one long sea voyage he made in his youth (see "Introduction," paragraph 3) sufficed to convince him that his reluctance to leave Paris and France had been well-founded. . . . In the first stanza of segment VII, the word "horreur" in a misanthropic context obviously denotes an objective loathsomeness (hence the rendition "filth"), rather than a subjective feeling of revulsion or disgust. . . . In stanzas 5 and 6 of segment VII, Baudelaire borrows freely from the concepts and language of Tennyson's poem "The Lotos-Eaters." In segment VIII, however, his mood is in striking contrast to that of Tennyson's "Crossing the Bar," as the two poets employ the same nautical metaphor for approaching death.

"Romantic Sunset": "Brink" sounds more appropriately ominous than would "edge" or "bank." "Fen" is preferred over "marsh,"swamp" or "bog" for its intrinsic musicality and for its alliterative value in this context. . . . "Imprévus" could be rendered more directly as "unforeseen" or "unexpected"; but the active-voice "startling" tends to sharpen the sensual imagery of this line. . . . "Clammy," added primarily for meter, also helps to evoke the final shudder to which the entire sestet has been building up.

"To a Malabar Girl": Although the young Baudelaire never made it to India's Malabar Coast on his one sea voyage (see "Introduction," paragraph 3), he probably encountered young women like this protagonist on the island of La Réunion. . . . Since it appears to be impossible to work both "bananas" and "pineapples" smoothly into line 10, the former have reluctantly been replaced by "mangoes."

"Retrospect": The word "encor" in line 4 is not a typographical error, but a non-standard spelling of "encore" often used by poets for concision, since it reduces by one the number of counted syllables.

INDEX OF TITLES

191

INDEX OF FIRST LINES (French)

ABOUT THE TRANSLATOR

Born the only son of a school administrator in northwestern Ohio, Kendall Lappin evinced early on a strong affinity for the interplay of languages. After majoring in French and Spanish at DePauw University and achieving fluency in French at Middlebury College, he taught high school language courses (including English) in Fairfield, Illinois until the outbreak of World War II. Upon graduation from the Navy's Japanese Language School in 1944, he served as a junior officer in the Pacific theater. At war's end he was assigned to the U. S. Naval Academy, to teach foreign languages to the midshipmen; soon thereafter he converted to civilian faculty status and made teaching at Annapolis his career, adding (in 1954) a Middlebury M. A. degree in Russian to his qualifications. Since his retirement in 1976 he has been active in literary translation—mostly poetry—from French to English.